3605543773

D1151609

The Team around the Child:
Multi-Agency Working in the Early Years

RuN
HT

The Team around the Child:
Multi-Agency Working in the Early Years

Edited by Iram Siraj-Blatchford,
Karen Clarke and Martin Needham

362·
7
TEA

tb

Trentham Books

Stoke on Trent, UK and Sterling, USA

1 8 MAY 2007

Trentham Books Limited
Westview House   22883 Quicksilver Drive
734 London Road   Sterling
Oakhill   VA 20166-2012
Stoke on Trent   USA
Staffordshire
England ST4 5NP

© 2007 Iram Siraj-Blatchford, Karen Clarke and Martin Needham

All rights reserved. No part of this publication may be reproduced or transmitted in any form or by any means, electronic or mechanical including photocopying, recording or any information storage or retrieval system, without prior permission in writing from the publishers.

First published 2007

British Library Cataloguing-in-Publication Data
A catalogue record for this book is available from the British Library

ISBN-13: 978 1 85856 418 0

Designed and typeset by Trentham Print Design Ltd, Chester and printed in Great Britain by Hobbs the Printers Ltd, Hampshire.

Contents

Foreword

Dame Gillian Pugh

Multi-agency working in the early years is not a new phenomenon. The concept of combining the education and welfare of young children and of providing broadly-based support for them and their parents was central to the work of Robert Owen in Scotland in the early 1800s, as indeed it was to the McMillan sisters, who had such a influence on nursery education in England in the early 1900s. A holistic, community-based service was also behind the development of community schools and colleges in the 1920s – forerunners of today's extended schools. But, as the slow and limited growth of combined nursery centres in the 1970s and 1980s illustrates, working together across agencies is not easy, particularly when the bigger systems of service administration and of training continue to separate both professionals and the services that they provide into separate silos. This book is a timely reminder of what can be achieved when agencies come together to focus on children and families. Whilst much of what is happening today is not new in itself, it is the bringing together of so many different strands of policy development, service provision and training that will create a lasting impact.

When Prime Minister Tony Blair said at the launch of *Every Child Matters* (HMT, 2003) that this was the most important document relating to children for over thirty years, he was not exaggerating. Although many of the elements of *Every Child Matters* and the subsequent 2004 Childcare Act were not new, it was the breadth and overall vision of the new agenda that would require a massive paradigm shift on the part of all who work with children and their families. For the new focus was not to be on service providers but on children and families, and was not to be on inputs but on outcomes, and particularly on improving outcomes for all children and young people, and on reducing the gaps between those who do well and those who do not. Multi-agency working and integrated services might be the means of improving outcomes for children, but they were not to be the ends. Young children and their families do not see their needs for early education, health care, job or housing advice in separate silos, and neither should the professionals working with them. Multi-agency working was to be encouraged as the most effective way of responding to the needs of service users.

Many of the recent developments in early years provision pre-dated *Every Child Matters* and, indeed, were influential in its development. Sure Start local programmes, for example, which evolved out of the new Labour government's cross-department review of services for children under eight in 1998, were established to provide support for families in the early months and years of a child's life, with a strong emphasis on prevention; however they were also required to be set up in and by local communities, and to both employ and have on their management committee, representatives of health, education, social services, the voluntary sector and parents. At around the same time the 'early excellence centres' initiative was launched, building on the earlier combined nursery centres, with a focus on integrating education and care for young children, providing support for families, child and family health services, and support for other services such as childminder networks.

Every Child Matters and the 2004 Children Act were therefore building on good early years practice in their response to the failures in the system that were identified in Lord Laming's report on the death of Victoria Climbié. Five key themes were identified: building strong foundations in the early years; a stronger focus on parenting and families; earlier interventions and effective protection; better accountability and integration locally, regionally and nationally; and reform of the workforce. The overall aims can be summarised as improving outcomes for all children and narrowing the gap between those who do well and those who do not; improving and integrating universal services; more specialist help to promote opportunity and prevent problems; reconfiguring services around the child and family; and sharing responsibility for safeguarding children.

Children's Trusts are seen as the main catalysts at local authority level for achieving these aims, with specific proposals around integrated personnel – working in multi-agency teams, setting up multi-agency services (especially children's centres and extended schools), creating an integrated qualifications framework and a common core of skills and knowledge for all who work with children; integrated processes – the common assessment framework and a single database of information on all children; integrated systems – a single children and young people's plan and a joint commissioning framework; and inter-agency governance – a director of children's services and a lead member or elected councillor for children.

The Team Around the Child is firmly grounded in practice, but within a research and policy framework. Through the use of case studies and analysis, the chapters provide a snapshot of how some of these high level policy objectives are working out on the ground, in relation to services for young children and their families, and we are reminded of the importance of learning from existing models of provision, rather than starting from scratch or reinventing wheels. The authors draw on their personal experience to cover key issues for policy makers and practitioners alike: research on quality and effectiveness in early childhood services, safeguarding children, leading multi-agency teams, the ethical challenges of multi-agency working, the importance of sharing information and creating a shared vision, working in communities and with parents, creating a learning organisation that values reflective practice, and the importance of joint training. Although few of those working in the field are challenging the overall vision of Every Child Matters and the childcare strategy, and much has been achieved nationally in a very short time, the themes throughout this book reflect a wider body of research that points to both the value and the challenges of multi-agency working. The tensions and complexities of such work are many, including different status, pay and conditions; different qualifications and training routes; different value bases, cultures, ideologies and traditions; lack of commitment and support from senior management; the challenges of managing the size and pace of change and of changing the culture; and the amount of time that it takes to build up trust.

But there is a more positive note. This book and other studies of effective multi-agency working are remarkably consistent in the messages that they convey. Amongst these are the need for shared vision and purpose and realistic aims and objectives; the importance of strong and effective leadership and supportive management; the need for careful planning; the importance of clearly defined roles, responsibility and accountability; a good communications strategy; and opportunities for joint training in order to create a shared culture and to develop trust and respect.

This book will be of great value to policy makers and practitioners alike. As it shows so vividly, developing and maintaining good multi-agency working is not always easy, but, a team around the child, starting with the child, can create a service that is more responsive to the needs of individual children and their parents and which should give young children the best possible start in life.

Introduction: diversity in multi-agency working

Iram Siraj-Blatchford, Martin Needham and Karen Clarke

Following the Government's green paper *Every Child Matters* (DOH, 2003), the *Children Bill*, and *Every Child Matters: Next Steps* (DfES, 2004) and the Childcare Act (HMSO, 2006), much of this massive programme of change has been left to local development. We should therefore expect a wide range of structures and approaches to be implemented across the country. Local authorities are now required to integrate and improve access to their services and improve the outcomes of all children under five. The Childcare Act 2006 requires local authorities to ensure that services are 'sufficient' for their area. This leaves a great deal of scope for interpretation: should sufficiency include the provision of specialist services and quality issues as well as the long-standing commitment to deliver places for all three and four year-olds whose parents require a place?

The government's stated overall aims are to tackle child poverty, improve education and childcare for young children, raise standards, and provide greater support for parents in bringing up their children (Childcare Act 2006). These developments represent the most important changes to children's services in the last twenty years. They also represent the greatest challenges. A key part of achieving these outcomes is the on-going development of children's centres that integrate the provision of education, care, family support and health services. However, all staff working with young children will need to consider how to work more proactively towards early interventions that will promote positive outcomes for children. The change from 'child protection' to 'safeguarding children' is significant: it signals a desire to promote greater emphasis on the prevention of negative outcomes rather than supporting families only at crisis points. The *Every Child Matters* agenda encourages society to take a broader view of children in the context of their families and stresses the importance of addressing a range of family needs in collaboration with partners. A variety of multi-agency approaches are likely to be developed to serve the needs of children and families. This will contextualise the relationships between agencies and families and yet, at the same time, enable each family's need to be addressed specifically.

This book is of special interest to everyone involved in children's centres and in the development of multi-agency strategies across other early years provision. The book also supports those involved in the continuing process of developing the 'extended school'. This encompasses practitioners from a variety of disciplines including social workers, those working directly with children and their families, educators, managers, policy makers and advisors. The book is also intended to be a useful resource for both academics and students in further and higher education.

We editors are aware that there are overlaps and some repetition in the chapters if the book is read as a whole; this is intentional since this allows the chapters to be used in isolation, for instance by a student who might be writing an assignment on child protection. This allows readers to pick from the book similar perspectives of multi-agency work from single chapters, or compare and contrast perspectives from different chapters, depending on their specific requirements. For this same reason we have appended references to each chapter rather than at the end of the book.

Several of the chapters draw on single or small numbers of case studies where practitioners from different perspectives have been asked to reflect on the way that multi-agency working is impacting on their practice. We do not claim that any or all of these perspectives are wholly representative; if readers do have time to consider different chapters then a picture begins to emerge of the diversity of practice and thinking in relation to multi-agency working. The chapters offer insights into the nature of the discourse taking place between national and local level at this significant point in the development of children's services in England.

In chapter one Iram Siraj-Blatchford draws on research and existing high quality, integrated practice to indicate the reasons why so much attention is being focused on multi-agency, integrated provision for young children and support for them within their families. This chapter identifies key issues and debates that have emerged from existing integrated centres (often referred to during the 1970s-1990s as combined centres) and argues that we should be able to build from some firm foundations rather than starting from scratch. The author urges us to learn from existing good models of practice in integrating education with care, health and parent support; she identifies some of the main ingredients of these good models, such as staff training and attention to a core service for children and families to improve learning outcomes. She touches on some of the problems (which cannot be dealt with in depth in a book of this nature, which aims to show examples of good practice) related to staff qualifications and training which historically are also associated with problems related to staff pay and conditions of service.

In chapter two Margaret McCullough examines the ways in which child protection services in England are being developed and integrated in response to government guidelines. The chapter draws from case studies of two local authorities, one of which was identified as a 'pathfinder' in developing practice. The author brings us up to date on recent developments, exploring some of the key documents and initiatives, including the Common Assessment Framework. Clearly, distinctions are made between these concepts and the concrete progress that is being made 'on the ground'.

In chapter three Jenny French provides us with a comprehensive historical background to the development of multi-agency working. She asks the crucial question of how much we have progressed over the last 46 years. She notes that in terms of the eradication of disadvantage and child poverty little has been achieved. She argues that attitudes towards cooperative working must change for the current initiatives to be successful. We must not compromise the dedication and commitment to families of practitioners, but provide appropriate resources and effective leadership and management.

Chapter four draws upon published research and reflection from the first ten years of the National Childcare Strategy to illustrate how government policy has evolved from one of creating provision for young children, to one of developing 'quality' integrated, multi-disciplinary services. Martin Needham provides a case study to illustrate how one local authority is developing multi-agency working on an area basis as 'teams around the child'. The case study shows that reflection on policy changes can inform the development of multi-agency working structures and identify issues where those working in such contexts may find it especially helpful to focus attention.

In multi-agency work the possibilities for misunderstanding can be enormous and it is in this context that Judy Whitmarsh, in chapter five, provides readers with valuable practical suggestions for resolving problems. She explores many of the major ethical challenges to multi-agency working including the critical issues of information sharing and confidentiality. The chapter makes a strong case for leaders to be proactive in encouraging discussions of the issues before problems arise.

In chapter six Bernadette Duffy and Janice Marshall draw upon their experience of integrated centres over the last 25 years to look at the particularly demanding business of leading multi-agency teams. They identify many of the challenges and provide valuable suggestions on how these may be tackled. They also argue that there is a need for more effective and empowering leadership that offers unique opportunities to develop and support the development of leadership skills in colleagues, children and parents.

In chapter seven, Faye Stanley reviews established writings to justify the move towards more integrated practices. She draws upon the experience of three practitioners: an established children's centre manager, the deputy of a centre under development and a special school teacher who has gained extensive experience of multi-agency working. The author identifies some of the challenges for practitioners highlighted by research into effective multi-agency working.

Jenny Worsley's study in chapter eight is grounded firmly in the concrete experiences of a newly established children's centre. She offers a useful five-stage model for children's centres that are becoming learning communities, and numerous other practical suggestions for developing communities of practice.

In chapter nine Amanda French and Karen Clarke explore some of the different ways in which parents may be more fully involved in the work of children's centres and extended schools. Framing their discussion in terms of family literacy, language and numeracy programmes and wider family learning, they argue that multi-agency approaches provide fertile ground for the development of learning communities and more collaborative practice with parents.

Although each author is grounded in a different professional discipline, each of the chapters emphasises the value of multi-agency working to enhance provision for children and families. But each recognises some of the different components necessary to ensure that multi-agency working is effective. Some interesting common ideas emerge from the chapters. Most prominent is the need for partners to share information and ideas in order to develop and recognise shared values of practice, of which sound communication, a vision which is understood by all and effective leadership are of paramount importance.

References

DfES (2004) *Every Child Matters: Next Steps*. Nottingham: Department for Education and Science

Department of Health (2003) *Every Child Matters*. CM5860. London: Her Majesty's Stationery Office

HMSO (2006) *Childcare Act 2006*. London: Her Majesty's Stationery Office.

1

The case for integrating education with care in the early years

Iram Siraj-Blatchford

Provisions for under-five year olds in the UK have been and are extremely diverse. Provisions currently include local authority day nurseries and family centres, playgroups, private and workplace nurseries, child-minders, and children's centres. There are also local (education) authority and private nursery classes and schools, as well as a very large number of four-year-olds in infant school classes. As Peter Kingston observed, 'The jumbled world of early learning and care... contained 35 categories of provider at the last count' (*Education Guardian*, p2, 27.6.1995). In spite of recent changes, these various government departments, agencies, and interest groups also hold different aims and goals, they have different admissions criteria and hours of opening, and they are staffed by people – largely women – with different training, different levels of pay and different conditions of service (Pugh, 1992; Sylva, Siraj-Blatchford and Johnson, 1992, Ball, 1994).

To some extent these different services also cater for different groups of families and children. While independent and voluntary provision is more likely to be used by parents of socially advantaged children, those from disadvantaged backgrounds have been over-represented in local authority day nurseries, children's centres and nursery schools (Melhuish *et al*, 1999). Even within the state sector there have been important differences between the services provided. Day nurseries often provide whole day care and are administered and staffed by those with two years training with the primary emphasis being on young children's social and emotional development (Sylva, Siraj-Blatchford and Johnson, 1992). These day nurseries do not normally employ teachers. Maintained sector nursery classes and schools, by contrast, are administered and staffed by education workers with a graduate teaching qualification, they are often supported by nursery officers with two years training or a teaching assistant. The primary emphasis here is on young children learning through a quality curriculum. In the following pages I argue that within this tradition, the contribution of combined provision has been most significant. Effective educators have always accepted that they should care for and about the children in their charge. Similarly, most parents and professionals understand that caring for a child involves the encouragement of early learning. But the development of combined provisions, the first of which was set up over 30 years ago, was aimed from the start at providing a more flexible and integrated service to children and parents. The new integrated children's centres are modelled on this.

Developments in early childhood provision

Robust research evidence from the United States, like the High/Scope Perry pre-school programme (Schweinhart *et al*, 1993), and the English Effective Provision of Pre-school Education (EPPE) study (Sammons *et al*, 2002, 2003) has shown that high quality Foundation Stage provision can be of lasting benefit to children, particularly children from low socio-economic classes. Given the strength of this evidence it was not surprising that in 1997 a 'New' Labour Government embarked upon a radical programme of educational reform that included a major expansion of pre-school provision. But it is important to recognise that developments did not begin at that point. The development of combined centres predates these initiatives by many years, even if it is only now possible that their aspirations be realised at a national level through the Children's Centre agenda.

It was as early as in 1989 that the *House of Commons Education Select Committee on Educational Provision for the Under-Fives* (HMSO, 1989) recommended combined provision as the best way forward to meet the needs of families and children. The following year, the Rumbold Committee of Inquiry into the Educational Experiences Offered to Three-and-Four-Year-Olds, *Starting with Quality*: (DES, 1990) made similar recommendations which were in turn followed by the independent *StartRight* report published by the RSA in 1994. The National Association of Nursery Centres (NANC) was at that time the national body representing a network of support for combined centres. Their aims were:

> To promote high quality, fully integrated care and education in partnership
> with parents and carers. The Association believes in the value of working as

multi-disciplinary teams co-ordinating qualifications, experience and skills. (NANC, 1994)

StartRight recommended the development and increase of combined provisions for all children aged three and four whose parents wanted it (RSA, 1994). Following its success in the 1997 general election, the Labour Government established its Early Excellence Centre (EECs) programme with the first eleven combined centres designated by the autumn of 1997. By 1999 there were 29, and in February 2001 a green paper, *Building on Success*, announced the expansion of the programme to 100 EECs by 2004. By the autumn of 2003 there were 107. The reported success of the EECs pilot programme (Bertram *et al*, 2002) then coincided with the publication of the EPPE effectiveness findings, and both strongly informed the development of Government thinking reflected in the 2003 green paper *Every Child Matters* (HM Treasury, 2003). The 2003 Green Paper launched a major Children's Centre initiative which has now been further elaborated in the Government's ten year strategy (HM Treasury, 2004) which aims to have 3,500 children's centres in place by 2010 serving the most disadvantaged communities.

> The Government is establishing a network of Sure Start Children's Centres in disadvantaged areas, offering integrated early education and full day care, health services, and family and parenting support... Children's Centres will play a key role in supporting groups who are at risk as well as delivering mainstream childcare and education services. (HM Treasury, 2003, Section 2.6)

This is an ambitious programme and in its realisation there will be much to learn from the experiences of the pioneers of combined provision. Most of our combined centres had gained extensive experience of working in multi-professional teams and in a multi-agency context. As *Every Child Matters: Change for Children* notes, the delivery of more integrated services will require the newly formed children's centres to develop new ways of working. This will involve a significant culture change for staff 'used to working within narrower professional and service-based boundaries' (DfES, 2004, Section 3.18). But the advantages are substantial:

> Multi-disciplinary working helps to ensure that children, young people and their families are given swift and simple access to the complementary skills of a wide range of people working together. It is not about losing the benefit of individual specialisms, although joint working may lead to some re-modelling of roles. Multi-disciplinary teams can also secure well-focused access to more specialised support when that is necessary. (*op cit* Section 3.19)

Moreover, the creation of a singular inspection process and the ongoing development of the ECM agenda and children's centres enshrined in the 2006 Childcare Act will aid the realisation of a new, integrated vision, but it is far from an easy task and a huge effort and commitment will be required on the part of all professionals. The current discrepancies in contracts and training of staff will continue to be a recurrent issue here.

The role of qualified educators in the early years

As previously noted, the pre-school services that are currently available vary enormously in terms of staff training and in the services provided. In the development of effective multi-professional practice, leadership will therefore be crucial. The Children's Workforce Development Council (CWDC) has published a report on strategies and key targets for raising the proportion of the early years workforce with Level 3 qualifications, the equivalent of a nursery officer's training. They aim to see 70% of the early years workforce qualified to Level 3 by 2010.

The EPPE study found the quality of the learning environment provided (as identified by Early Childhood Environment Rating Scales (ECERS-E and R)) increased with the early years leaders' qualifications. The leaders with the highest early years qualifications were also found predominantly in the education rather than the care sector (i.e. in nursery schools and classes), and in combined centres (Taggart *et al*, 2000). Figure 1 below shows the mean ECERS scores (on a scale from 1 to 7) grouped according to the manager's early years qualification level, where level 5 is graduate, teacher trained. (Under the new workforce discussions qualification levels are changing, and graduates might well be described as levels 6 or 7). Note that the ECERS have been shown to correlate with children's cognitive and social developmental outcomes, and a clear trend is shown in which the quality of the environment

Figure 1: ECERS-R and ECERS-E means by manager qualification

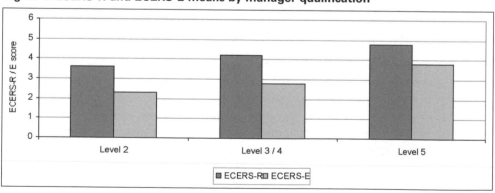

increases with the level of qualification. The positive learning effects identified by EPPE include social-behavioural as well as cognitive effects and these effects were most pronounced for the most disadvantaged and underachieving children (working class, some ethnic minority groups, special needs etc). Statistical analysis of variance has revealed that these trends are significant on both ECERS measures ($p<0.01$).

The EPPE study found that variations in the effectiveness of individual settings were often greater than variations between different types of provider. However, children were found to benefit significantly more when they attended local authority combined centres (Sammons *et al*, 2003ab). EPPE also found that settings with better qualified workers, and especially those with a good proportion of trained teachers on the staff, showed higher quality provision, and their children made greater academic progress and better social/behavioural gains (Sylva *et al*, 2004 p56). The qualitative case studies conducted in the Researching Effective Pedagogy in the Early Years (REPEY) project confirmed this, showing that:

> Qualified staff in the most effective settings provide children with more experience of academic activities (especially literacy and mathematics) and they encourage children to engage in activities with higher cognitive challenge. While we found that the most highly qualified staff provided the most direct teaching, we found that they were the most effective in their interactions with the children, encouraging the most sustained shared thinking. Further we found that less qualified staff are significantly better pedagogues when they are supervised by qualified teachers. (Siraj-Blatchford *et al*, 2002, p11)

Unfortunately only 12% of the current early years workforce is qualified to level 4/5; this compares to 80% of primary school teachers qualified to level 5 (Daycare Trust, April 2005).

If we are to achieve better learning outcomes it is therefore essential that we provide more and better qualified educators, especially teachers with an appropriate early years training. Many of the day care centres provided previously by social services integrated some education with their childcare but EPPE found that the quality of the educational provisions made by the combined centres provided by local education authorities (LEAs) were higher. With the change of LEAs to Local Authority children's services it will be important to monitor whether educational input is adequate:

> The LEA nursery schools which had changed from 'education only' to 'integrated' centres (offering full day care and parental support) usually scored

highest of all. Furthermore, adding 'education' to more traditional local authority day care settings through the addition of just one teacher or a peripatetic teacher was not associated with higher quality. EPPE found that settings integrating care and education had high scores only when there was a good balance between 'care' and 'education' in terms of staff qualifications. This implies that the successful integration of care and education is related to the proportion of staff with 'educational' qualifications. (Sylva *et al*, 2004, p16)

Teaching and learning matters

Evidence from the EPPE/REPEY studies (see Siraj-Blatchford *et al*, 2002; 2003) has highlighted some key characteristics of sound practice that will support good child outcomes as stated in Every Child Matters. The studies draw on a wealth of data collected from case studies of effective practice, that is practice which yielded better child outcomes. The case studies reflect the major types on early years, group provision eg playgroup, reception classes, maintained nurseries, private day nurseries and local authority daycare. Below we highlight some of the key features.

- Settings gained better outcomes for children where there were higher levels in terms of quantity and quality of the teacher/adult-planned and initiated focused, small group work.

- Good settings had sound leadership, good communication and shared consistent ways of working amongst the staff and a higher number of teachers.

- Most of the better case study settings created a good balance between adult planning and free-choice for children in their provision (Nursery Schools/classes, Combined Centres).

- Open-ended questioning does appear to be associated with better cognitive achievement.

- Settings where staff adopted discipline/behaviour policies that involved them in supporting children to rationalise and talk through their conflicts had better social outcomes. In settings which are less effective on this outcome our observations show that there is often no follow-up on children's misbehaviour, and on many occasions children are distracted from interfering with other children, or simply instructed to stop.

- The qualitative analysis of our teacher observations also appears to show an association between curriculum differentiation and matching in terms of cognitive challenge, and sustained shared thinking. The qualitative evidence suggests that the better the setting does on each of these dimensions of good pedagogic practice, the more cognitively effective it will be.

- Our findings suggest that where staff shared educational aims with parents, and encouraged pedagogic efforts at home, good child outcomes were established.

- Three conditions for learning were identified in the literature review: adult and child involvement, the identification of foundations for construction, and instruction. Our analyses of the qualitative data substantiate this and our research has shown that adult-child interactions that involve some element of sustained shared thinking may be especially valuable in terms of child development.

- In the settings where this sort of shared thinking is most encouraged by staff, the interactions are often child-initiated and they provide a better basis for learning right across the curriculum.

- The socio-dramatic play of the home corner provides a particularly useful context for such interactions, and we found many incidents of staff getting directly involved in children's play and stimulating their imagination by open questioning.

- We found examples of practitioners whose knowledge and understanding of the particular curricular area under study was inadequate, and this led to missed opportunities or uncertain outcomes; this was particularly the case for the direct teaching of phonics. This suggests the need for more depth in early years staff education in the area of pedagogical subject knowledge. Teachers were better at this than less qualified staff.

- Children had better outcomes in settings where we found a good deal of evidence in support of formative assessment.

- EPPE findings (Sammons *et al*, Technical Paper 2) have shown that children who are taken to the library, who read with their parents, who play with letters and numbers and who sing songs and rhymes at home have a head start even at age 3 on cognitive scores. What staff did with the parents and children to encourage these behaviours was more prevalent in better settings.

- Less effective staff emphasised parents' needs above those of their children, rather than seeing the needs of children and parents as different but complementary. They also promoted social development and support above educational development, rather than seeing these as complementary.

- Involvement in learning activities at home and parent involvement in decision-making, leadership, and governance have been shown to be associated with better academic achievement (Epstein, 1991). Our findings show that it is the involvement in learning activities that is more closely associated with better cognitive attainment in the early years. All fourteen of the settings encouraged parents to read with their children, but those that had higher qualified staff encouraged continuity of learning at home and had better cognitive outcomes.

- Parents felt that settings which were sensitive, responsive and consistent (in terms of staff) were more effective, and this links well with the research literature on good practice (Bowman *et al*, 2001).

Learning from combined nursery centres to develop children's centres

Among the first combined centres to provide fully integrated provision in terms of education, childcare and family support were the Hillfields Centre in Coventry which first opened in 1971, the Gamesley Centre which opened in Glossop in 1973 and the Penn Green Centre which opened in 1983 in Corby. In the mid 1990s the National Association of Nursery Centres estimated that there were approximately 50-70 combined centres in the UK. At that time neither the Department for Education nor the Department for Health and Social Services kept any record of the precise number. Combined centres provided for family support, and catered for children below three years as well as the three- and four-year-olds provided for in alternative pre-school settings.

Their aim was to draw together family support, health, child care and education under one integrated system. Combined centres therefore aimed to provide the greatest continuity of experience between home and school for children from 0-5 years, and to involve parents fully in the process. Many of these centres have been widely recognised as 'centres of excellence' within the early years community and they have been visited regularly by early childhood educators in the UK and from overseas. Thus four of the seven combined centres included in the stratified random sample drawn by EPPE were designated Early Excellence Centres (EECs) as part of the Labour Government's

1997 strategy for raising standards and educational opportunities, supporting families, and addressing child poverty.

It was intended that each EEC should offer a one-stop-shop where families and children could gain access to high quality integrated care and education services delivered by multi-agency partners within one centre or by a network of centres.

Combined centres have normally been administered by local education departments and there have always been some problems associated with the differences in the conditions of service and responsibilities of the education and care staff that have worked within them. But these difficulties should not be exaggerated: in an early study of such centres the difficulties were also found to be reflected in other services and not confined solely to combined nursery centres (Ferri *et al*, 1981). The integrated nature of these centres has drawn greater attention to some of the problems which also exist in these wider contexts.

The integrated, holistic approach that is offered in combined provision has been shown to be more flexible and responsive to local needs (Murphy, 1989; Yates, 1991, Siraj-Blatchford, 1995). Drawing upon the specialist skills and expertise of teachers and nursery officers, combined centres aimed to integrate partnership and support for parents and families and provide a continuity of care and learning between the home and school.

In many combined centres each member of staff took responsibility related to their specialist area of expertise. It would be unrealistic to expect any worker to be expert at all the roles that centres demand. Economically, and in terms of time and resources, the recognition and utilisation of comparative advantage was seen as a sensible policy. While all staff received in-service training in care, health and education, their initial training was also valued. This must remain the case in children's centres.

The development of multi-professional teams
Many combined nursery centres were fortunate in being able to borrow from the best practice of social services and educational provision in terms of multi-professional working. As pilot EECs, both the Gamesley (Glossop) and Thomas Coram (London) Children's Centres were included in the national evaluation of Early Excellence initiatives in 2002 (Siraj-Blatchford *et al*, 2002a, 2002b). The Gamesley Centre was managed by a head teacher, with a qualified social worker with NNEB qualifications as a deputy. The management team also included three team leaders, two of whom were qualified teachers

and the other an NNEB family support worker. Each team had four nursery officers who were also family support workers. The deputy and the family support workers were all employed by the Social Services department, the head and teachers by the Education department. The centre is proud of its contribution towards reducing child protection referrals and its support for parents' social networks. At the time of the evaluation, 11% of the local population were accessing some form of adult education at the centre.

While the Thomas Coram EEC occupies a separate building to the Coram Parents Centre, they are immediately adjacent and share a joint governing body which includes all the agencies with a stake in the centres. This group sought to ensure that the services of the different agencies were delivered in an integrated fashion. The two parts of the centre joined together for INSET days and monthly centre development meetings. The focus for these sessions was joint areas of work or interest as outlined in the centre development plan, for example work with 0-3s, music making, parental partnership and community involvement.

Both Gamesley and Coram provided a wide range of counselling services, parents' classes, supported parents' groups and outreach activities. At Coram a common progression was identified, from parents being contacted by the outreach workers or young parents project workers, through sometimes attending groups in their children's school or the nursery, then moving to informal and then more formal accredited classes in the Parents Centre:

> Seventeen parents gained employment this year as a direct result of their involvement in the Parents Centre, many more have moved on to college, and this positive outcome has only been possible as a result of the sensitive (and sometimes slow) process of initial engagement. (Siraj-Blatchford *et al*, 2002b)

As Bertram *et al* (2002) have argued, successful multi-professional practice requires the development of shared philosophies and agreed working principles:

> A successful team is one that demonstrates professionalism, shared beliefs, common identity and vision and a breadth of expertise and skills, and feels secure enough within the management system to take on new activities without fear and to operate within a professional climate which balances openness to new ideas with pragmatic critique... Successful practice seems to involve a relaxation of professional boundaries and the development of a non-judgemental but highly professional and principled environment. (*op cit* p10)

Most combined centres offered their staff regular supervision and support sessions, and one-to-one discussion of individual progress. In terms of training, centres usually had access to LEA in-service training on curriculum, assessment and reporting to parents. Social services also provided centre staff with training on issues of child protection, home liaison and the care of under-threes and, because of the many agencies the staff were in contact with, they often built up good relations with health visitors, social workers, speech therapists and others. In every case, these helped in developing the staff's awareness of areas important to both children and their parents.

The recent *Early Years Foundation Stage* (EYFS) has put emphasis on teaching and formative assessment and documentation through the development and learning record and common assessment framework (Sect 3.4). No sensible curriculum is possible without careful planning based on observation, assessment and record-keeping. Children's knowledge, concepts, attitudes, skills and feelings must be taken into account and educators can learn about these through careful observation and regular discussion about the observations; these in turn will help to determine the effectiveness of the curriculum on offer. Assessment also includes the monitoring and development of the centre as a whole, relationships with parents, and staff development. Having teachers on the staff certainly helps and they are usually the ones who take a leadership role in planning the curriculum programmes and supporting staff in developing learning activities. An awareness of the way that children have learnt at home through their 'natural curriculum' is vital, as is a strong understanding of the kind of curriculum children are likely to face in their reception year in school. All centre staff should contribute towards providing an essential continuity between home, the centre and the school. It is also essential that staff understand the role of play in children's development and of the role of adults in facilitating play which develops children's social, emotional, cognitive, physical and creative aptitudes.

The EYFS emphasises the importance of assessment for learning, documenting children's progress and the EYFS profile. From birth, all children should have a development and learning record to which parents and practitioners contribute, and which will go with them from setting to setting. Some children may have additional needs and, therefore, might benefit from an additional assessment so that practitioners can support their development and learning better. The Common Assessment Framework (CAF) helps professionals from all agencies to work together on this.

Key workers and lead practitioners

Rouse and Griffin (1992) argue that younger children need intimate relationships with a significant, responsive adult. Centres can strengthen and support children's development and learning by establishing a day-to-day, one-to-one link for parents and children. This can be with a particular educator who is responsible for monitoring the quality of care and education a child receives. Primary educators should have a key responsibility to liaise with the parent/carer, to collate records of the child's development and to act as a significant reference point for information on the child and her family. This will be especially important where, for instance, a child protection issue arises or home visiting is needed. For most children, the lead professional role may be best fulfilled by someone from the service who has the most contact with the child day to day.

A lead professional acts as a single point of contact for a child and their family when a range of services are involved and an integrated response is required. The lead professional supports the child and family in getting the help they need and the role is intended to reduce overlap and inconsistency between practitioners and services. The lead professional should ensure that the child and family get appropriate interventions when needed, which are well planned, regularly reviewed and effectively delivered. The role of lead professional can be taken on by a variety of practitioners working with children as the role is defined by functions and skills, rather than by particular professional or practitioner groupings. Most combined settings have extensive experience of working with a key worker system. This approach means that parents can access a link member of staff who they know and trust.

Partnership with parents

Family and community involvement is a vital part of good practice for many centres; among other centres doing an excellent job in this respect, the Penn Green Centre in Corby has become world famous for this. Many centres aim to provide parent 'empowerment' by increasing parents' confidence in themselves and in their parenting and teaching skills. After a self-awareness course held by staff for parents at the Hillfields Nursery Centre, all the parents who took part reported a gain in confidence. This was also evident in the parents' increased involvement in the Centre and for some, their advancement to further and higher education.

At the Camrose Nursery Centre in Northampton, the parent-friendly ethos has encouraged parents to set up their own support networks including discussions over weekly lunches, keep-fit classes and educational events for small groups of children, for example nature trails.

Developing partnerships with parents is a key feature of the Coram centre's work. Centre staff work in partnership with parents in a number of ways:

- as partners in individual children's learning and development (taken from the Assessing and Implementing Policy)
- as partners in developing the centre curriculum (evidence seen in their SRB Parental Participation Programme file)
- as partners in developing centre policies and practice (as seen in minutes of Parents Forums governing body and committee minutes)

All parents are aware that the quality of their own lives is improved, in some cases dramatically, by the services provided by the Thomas Coram Centre. In addition to safe and secure child care, they cite from the nursery courses, increased knowledge about children's speech and language, about nutrition, and about behaviour problems. From the CPC, personal gains are mostly described as enhanced confidence and self-esteem, feeling good, 'enjoying life and learning from it', and being challenged; children are seen to benefit enormously from the crèche facility. Most centre users feel they have made new friends, although their view of this varies according to family circumstances. In some respondents' experience, the new friendships are a source of emotional support and advice.

The examples are endless, but again the evidence should be based not only upon policies but also upon daily practices, particularly those which support parents in parenting skills and those which involve parents in the governance and decision-making procedures. These could be related to the curriculum, inspections or behaviour policies, amongst other things. Where parents themselves come forward with innovative ideas and the questions which matter to them is a sign of very good practice in which centres have created a respectful, power-sharing ethos. Centres need to reflect upon and respond to the struggles within the local community, so that, for example, if racist attacks occur, they have a role in providing information for parents on their rights and on where they can go for further support. (See appendix 1 at the end of this chapter for a case study on one integrated, fully combined centre.)

Conclusions: the continuity of care and learning

The quality of care and learning are of the utmost importance to both children's development and to the trust that parents develop in a centre's staff. Much has been written from an education perspective about the quality of child-to-child interaction and about adult-child interaction. Less has been written about the value of adult-adult interaction, be it with parents or with other staff. Centres are busy places and unless this area of quality is well planned for and regularly monitored it can easily become intuitively exercised by some rather than carefully applied by all.

Management matters: centres require a unique form of management, and perhaps that's why so many centre managers show a flair for creativity and innovation. Managing a multi-professional team and attending to the variety of support services involved as well as the children and parents can be very demanding. One of the centres I know has a staff of over thirty working flexitime, and over 250 children on roll. Most centres are open fifty weeks of the year. This is very different to a nursery class with 46 children part-time, a teacher, and one nursery officer, or to a day care centre with nursery officers and children. The nearest form of comparable management would probably be the community school. Most managers have little training for their role, but the nature of the work usually leads managers to adopt styles which are more democratic than hierarchical and which focus on good communication skills (Siraj-Blatchford and Manni, 2007).

Of course there is much more to quality in combined centres than has been mentioned in this chapter. If the child is at the heart of the learning and development process, with the recognition that families are an integral part of this, and that families are also in need of support, then surely any future early years expansion must consider services that take the parents' role seriously and invest in them as one important way forward.

Families are under increasing stress in both urban and rural areas and the rise in poverty has meant that over four million young children in the UK today live in poverty stricken households (Kumar, 1993; Hirsch, D, 2006). More than one in three children is now in a single parent household. Wherever children's centres are, the issue of quality is vital, and quality can vary in any service some of the previous issues therefore need to be considered in order to provide a quality service, in fact, an equality service.

References
Ball, C. (1994) *StartRight: the Importance of Early Learning,* RSA, London.

Bertram, T., Pascal, C., Bokhari, C., Gasper, M. and Holtermann, S. (2002) *Early Excellence Centre Pilot Programme Second Evaluation Report 2000-2001*, DfES Research Report No 361, London, HMSO

Bowlby, J. (1988) *A Secure Base: Parent-Child Attachment and Healthy Human Development.* London: Routledge; New York: Basic Books

Bowman, B., Donovan, S. and Burns, M. (Eds.) (2001) *Eager to Learn: Educating our Pre-schoolers.* Washington D.C: National Academy Press

Daycare Trust (2005) *More Work Needed On Workforce Strategy*, Paper accessed April 2005 at: http://www.daycaretrust.org.uk/article.php?op=Print&sid=248

Department of Education and Science (DES) (1990) *Starting with Quality: Report of the Committee of Inquiry into the Educational Experiences Offered to Three-and-Four-Year-Olds* (Rumbold Report), London, HMSO

Department for Education and Science (DfES) (2004) *Every Child Matters: Change for Children*, DfES-1110-2004, London, HMSO

Ferri, E., Birchall, D., Gingell, V. and Gipps, C. (1981) *Combined Nursery Centres: A New Approach to Education and Day Care*, Macmillan Press, London.

Her Majesty's Treasury (2003) *Every Child Matters* (Green Paper), London, TSO

Her Majesty's Treasury (2004) *Choice for parents, the best start for children: a ten year strategy for childcare*, London, HMSO

Hirsch, D. (2006) *What will it take to end child poverty?* York, Joseph Rowntree Trust.

HMSO (1989) House of Commons Education Select Committee (chaired by Timothy Raison) Educational Provision for the Under-Fives , HMSO, London.

Kumar, V. (1993) *Poverty and Inequality in the UK. Effects on Children*, National Children's Bureau, London.

Melhuish, E., Sylva, K., Sammons, P., Siraj-Blatchford, I., Taggart, B., Dobson, A., Jeavons. M., Lewis, K., Morahan. M., and Sadler. S. (1999) *The Effective Provision of Pre-School Education (EPPE) Project:* Technical Paper 4 – Parent, family and child characteristics in relation to type of pre-school and socio-economic differences, London: DfES/Institute of Education, University of London.

Murphy, L. (1989) The Combined Nursery Centre, B.Phil. thesis, Open University, School of Education.

NANC, (1994) Aims and Philosophy, from papers held by Siraj-Blatchford, I., London, Institute of Education, University of London

Pugh, G. (1992) *Contemporary Issues in the Early Years,* Paul Chapman and National Children's Bureau, London

Rouse, D. and Griffin, S. (1992) 'Quality for the Under-Threes' in Pugh, G. (Ed.) *op cit.*

Sammons, P., Sylva, K., Melhuish, E. C., Siraj-Blatchford, I., Taggart, B. (1999) *The Effective Provision of Pre-School Education (EPPE) Project: Technical Paper 2: Characteristics of the Effective Provision of Pre-School Education (EPPE) Project Sample at Entry to the Study*, (1999) London: DfES/Institute of Education, University of London.

Sammons, P., Sylva, K., Melhuish, E. C., Siraj-Blatchford, I., Taggart, B. and Elliot, K. (2003a), *The Effective Provision of Pre-School Education (EPPE) Project: Technical Paper 8a – Measuring the Impact of Pre-School on Children's Cognitive Development over the Pre-School Period*. London: DfES/Institute of Education, University of London.

Sammons, P., Sylva, K., Melhuish, E. C., Siraj-Blatchford, I., Taggart, B. and Elliot, K. (2003b), *The Effective Provision of Pre-School Education (EPPE) Project: Technical Paper 8b – Measuring the Impact of Pre-School on Children's Social/Behavioral Development over the Pre-School Period*. London: DfES/Institute of Education, University of London.

Schweinhart, L.J., Barnes, H.V. and Weikart, D.P. (1993). *Significant Benefits: The High/Scope Perry Pre-school Study through Age 27*. Michigan: High/Scope Educational Research Foundation.

Siraj-Blatchford, I. (1994) *The Early Years: Laying the Foundations for Racial Equality,* Trentham Books, Stoke on Trent.

Siraj-Blatchford, I. (1995) 'Expanding Combined Nursery Provision: Bridging the Gap between Care and Education' in Gammage, P. and Meighan, R. (Eds) *Early Childhood Education: The Way Forward.* Nottingham: Education Now Books

Siraj-Blatchford, I. (1999). 'Early childhood pedagogy, practice, principles and research' in P. Mortimore (Ed) *Understanding Pedagogy and its Impact on Learning.* London: Paul Chapman.

Siraj-Blatchford, I. (2002a) Final annual evaluation report of the Gamesley Early Excellence Centre. Unpublished report, University of London, Institute of Education

Siraj-Blatchford, I. (2002b) Final annual evaluation report of the Thomas Coram Early Excellence Centre. Unpublished report, University of London, Institute of Education

Siraj-Blatchford, I and Manni, L. (2007) *Effective Leadership in the Early Years Sector (ELEYS) study.* London, Institute of Education

Siraj-Blatchford, I., Sylva, K., Muttock., S., Gilden, R. and Bell, D. (2002) *Effective Pedagogy in the Early Years*, Research Report 356DfES

Siraj-Blatchford, I., Sylva, K., Taggart, B., Sammons, P., and Melhuish, E. (2003). *EPPE case studies Technical Paper 10.* University of London, Institute of Education/DfES

Sylva, K., Siraj-Blatchford, I. and Johnson, S. (1992) 'Top-down Pressures of the National Curriculum on Pre-school Education in the UK', *International Journal of Early Childhood* (OMEP), Vol. 24, No. 1, pp. 41-51.

Sylva, K., Melhuish, E. C., Sammons, P., Siraj-Blatchford, I. and Taggart, B. (2004) *The Effective Provsion of Pre-School Education (EPPE) Project: Final Report.* London: DfES/Institute of Education, University of London.

Taggart, B., Sylva, K., Siraj-Blatchford, I., Melhuish, E. C., Sammons, P. and Walker-Hall, J. (2000), *The Effective Provision of Pre-School Education (EPPE) Project: Technical Paper 5 – Characteristics of the Centres in the EPPE Sample: Interviews.* London: DfEE/Institute of Education, University of London.

Yates, D. (1991) *Staff Skills Develop in Line with Changes at Hillfields Nursery Centre to Provide a Family Service for Children Within the Family*, CPQS dissertation, Hillfields Nursery Centre.

Appendix: Reflective task

This case study (like any case study) is unique, but it will have features associated with its practice that are illuminating or where some comparison might be drawn with your own work. Consider how the case study compares to your own experience or expectations of multi-agency working.

Case Study: An effective centre that combines education with care and health

This case study focuses on the provision offered to three- to five-year-old children within a combined Early Excellence Centre situated in a multi-ethnic suburb of a large city (it is now a Children's Centre). The Centre was one of twelve settings selected for qualitative analysis in a stratified random of effective centres in the EPPE (Siraj-Blatchford *et al*, 2002; 2003) study.

Location, accommodation and intake

The Centre first opened in the 1970s and was nominated by the DfES as an Early Excellence Centre in the late 1990s (Ofsted). It is in an area of high social deprivation that has been described by the local press as 'the toughest area of the city'. Recent attempts have been made to improve the environment with an increase in public amenities and some property refurbishment. The few local shops satisfy basic needs but access to supermarkets situated further away poses problems for those without transport (field notes). The Centre has always been registered as a nursery school with the DfES.

The Centre is purpose-built to provide, under one roof, nursery provision from birth to 5 years for 50 weeks a year. It is designed to provide integrated care and education including extensive parental support, and is used by over 220 children each week and their families (information booklet).

Although the Centre is open between 8.00 am and 5.00 pm most children, including those in the case study, attend between 9.00 am and 3.30 pm and even these times are very flexible. It is closed to children during the last week of August and the first week of September to prepare for the new intake and to allow for staff turnover (field notes). The services are designed to respond flexibly to families' needs and include a crèche, parent and toddler groups, toy library, speech therapy, medical support and nursery education (Ofsted, 2000).

The children are organised according to age into three separate departments or 'teams' each with their separate accommodation. Other rooms serve to support these teams with administration offices, kitchens, bathrooms, laundry room, staff room, meeting and training rooms. The accommodation for the 3-4+ year old children occupies a large L-shaped room divided by screens into smaller areas with access to a large outdoor space.

The outdoor area is well resourced with a covered area, grass and hard surfaced areas, a grassy hill, a soft area with climbing frame and slide, a wooden train, a vegetable garden and a shed for storing equipment. There are also shrubs and trees and the area is well maintained. The bathroom is shared with younger children from another area (centre plans, observations).

Most of the local community live in rented accommodation on the nearby social housing estates, with the tower blocks providing homes for the more transient population. There are also some families living in privately owned homes (field notes). The unemployment rate of the area is 13.8%, which is high compared to the 4% unemployment figure for the city as a whole (head of centre interview).

The intake reflects the local community in terms of socio-economic make-up and ethnicity. There are 44 children on roll in the unit, of whom seventeen are from single parent families (38.63%), one child is in care and 25 children have free meals (56.83%) (field notes). Many children have low or very low levels of language skills on entry and a significant proportion have a range of other special needs (Ofsted, 2000).

Forty of these children (90.90%) have attended the Centre previously in one or both of the other two teams for younger children. The Centre offers a flexible programme of places according to the needs of individual families (field notes).

Original child placement is obtained by parental request and/or referral by the Health Department, Social Services or Pre-school Services. Decisions about allocation of places are made by a Centre Management Committee representing centre staff, Social Services, Education and Health Departments, parents, the local community, local providers and business links personnel (information booklet). Admission is granted according to applicants' needs in educational and emotional terms, whether they are on the 'at risk' register and the level of involvement with Social Services (field notes).

Philosophy

The Centre is committed to providing an integrated inter- and multi-agency service of quality day care provision for the children and families in the local community and to enhancing their educational achievements and extend future opportunities. It believes in acknowledging the key role of parents in the healthy development and learning of their children and aims to involve them in these processes at an early stage. Equal opportunities are given a high priority and are made visible in all aspects of the institution. The Centre staff believe in being sensitive to changing community needs and responding appropriately. Finally, it aims to be an establishment that values and empowers all adults and seeks to do this by encouraging and appreciating contributions made by everyone towards its on-going development, providing continuous professional development for staff and disseminating good practice (information booklet).

Funding

Funding is complex as monies are not received exclusively from a delegated LEA budget but from a number of sources. At the time of the Ofsted inspection 48% came from the LEA and the rest from eight different grant sources. These included private benefactors, grants from local community resources, Early Excellence Centre support from DfES, and European funds such as the Social Regeneration Budget (induction booklet).

The total budget is 'very well managed' by the Head (Ofsted, 2000) who receives help from the LEA Finance Team and a Senior Finance Officer who is a member of the Senior Management Team. The LEA is also responsible for administering the Centre (information booklet).

Staffing

There are 54 members of staff working at the Centre, 34 of whom work part-time. All are female. They are appropriately qualified and are drawn from a variety of disciplines, including teachers, nursery officers, a health practitioner, under 3s' special needs workers, language support workers, parent home visitors, toy library workers and a portage worker, as well as administrative and support staff (Ofsted, 2000).

The core staff for the 3-5s room is two qualified teachers, four nursery officers, a 0.5 ethnic minority support teacher, a part time bi-lingual assistant and two learning support assistants. There are usually a number of other part time and voluntary workers assisting at any one time. Students from a range of disciplines – social workers, NVQ trainees, nurses and teachers – may also be present (information booklet) as well as occasional students from overseas (observations). It was observed during the case study that a significant number of staff were engaged to provide cover and ratios were low a lot of the time, for example 1:5 (field notes summary).

Responsibilities, retention and relationships

All the staff working in the Centre are of white UK heritage except for two nursery officers who are of minority ethnic heritage. The room co-ordinator, who is also the Special Educational Needs Co-ordinator (SENCO) for the 2-4+ year olds, has worked at the centre for ten years; she is qualified to BA and PGCE (Post Graduate Certificate in Education – qualified teacher) level. She is responsible for the general management of the unit and for facilitating the team in planning daily and weekly activities. This is done during the planning meetings held between 3.45 and 4.15 pm every day.

The other full-time teacher, who has been in post for a year, is leaving to work in a primary school and will be replaced in the new academic year. She has a BA and PGCE and is also Montessori trained. The Ethnic Minority Achievement Grant (EMAG) teacher has worked 0.5 in the room for three years although she works full time at the Centre on a range of projects. She also has BA and PGCE qualifications.

There are currently five nursery workers covering four posts (two job-share). Of these the longest serving member (26 years) is the only one without formal qualifications: all the others have NVQ either 2 or 3. At the time of the case study the two learning support assistants (LSAs) were both graduates (both were leaving at the end of the year to pursue PGCE courses).

The stability in the 2-5s area improved with the appointment of the Centre's SENCO to unit co-ordinator in December 1999. She has worked at the Centre for ten years and is a keen supporter of the philosophy of the Head and Senior Management Team (SMT). Three of the nursery officers have worked in the Centre for five, six and eight years. One is on a one-year contract to cover maternity leave.

Key worker responsibilities

The Centre has a key worker system to achieve the consistency and continuity in day-care and education to which it believes children are entitled (policy document). Key worker staff are expected to be fully aware of their responsibilities and understand how personalities and actions influence their effectiveness. The policy states that the Centre wants staff who are genuine and sensitive, who enjoy working with children and value their role as in supporting and bringing together a better understanding between child and family (policy document). Responsibilities include the day-to-day care of the children in their key groups including sitting and eating with them during lunchtime. Another important aspect to their work is to build relationships with the family and provide support when necessary. Key workers are also responsible for producing the individual records of achievement which are summarised (with the curriculum deputy) into Pupil Profiles. Information concerning individuals is fed to other team members to influence planning where necessary (field notes).

Normal pay and conditions do not apply to most of the teaching staff. Apart from the bilingual assistants and LSAs, staff members are expected to work from 8.15 am to 4.15 pm with holidays taken by arrangement (field notes). Although teachers are entitled to full holiday allocation, in reality they rarely find this possible. Flexibility of holiday times is offered as some compensation (manager interview 1). Only the Ethnic Minority Achievement Grant teacher (EMAG), who is paid from EMAG funding, takes the usual thirteen weeks' holiday per year.

Management and leadership

The Centre has no governing body but is steered by a supportive management committee made up of centre staff, Social Services, Education and Health Departments, parents, the local community, local providers and business links personnel (information booklet).

The Head of Centre manages the Centre through the Senior Management Team (SMT) consisting of herself and three Deputy Heads who are each responsible for one of the following areas: Curriculum and Training, Pastoral issues and Family Support. The team is supported by three other members, a Senior Finance Officer and two part-time clerical officers (information booklet). Ofsted identifies the management of the centre as a particular strength, grading it as 'excellent' and noting that 'this complex Centre is effectively led and managed by a very good management team' (Ofsted, 2000).

The Head of Centre has been involved with the Centre for 18 years. Her responsibilities are for the total management of the staff team and the services provided. The Deputy for Curriculum and Training has been in post since 1994. She is responsible for monitoring and evaluating the quality of children's learning and access to the curriculum across the whole Centre by supporting adults in their role in this process. She also takes the lead on providing training programmes for other providers in the LEA. The Pastoral Deputy, who has worked at the Centre for twelve years, has a background in Social Services day nurseries and supports the personal and social development of all children, families and staff. This includes outreach support and behaviour management. She is also involved with the Social Services Child Protection policy and works directly with families to deliver information, training and general support. She makes weekly links with health visitors and the Community Medical Officer. The third deputy has worked at the Centre for 24 years and has been in her present post since 1998. Her responsibility is to support families by working in partnership with parents to raise their self-esteem and parenting skills and liaising with external agencies. With a background in Social Services, she is also involved with the training programme of Social Work students and represents the Centre in the local Early Years Development and Childcare Partnership.

The size and complexity of the staff has led to a hierarchical structure, with the institution directed by the Head of Centre and supported by the SMT. Although the Centre recognises the importance of individuals within an institution and the power of teamwork, such a structure may diminish opportunities for widespread democratic decision-making. Delegating specific responsibility areas to three deputies sustains this top-down, yet efficient, model and seems to work effectively in this setting.

Although 44 children are on roll in the nursery unit, most of the children attend for two or two and a half days with some children attending four or four and a half days.

Allowing for a slight variation each day because of the different attendance patterns, the age mix is between three years ten months and four years nine months.

Parental Involvement

The Head of Centre is driven by a deeply-held and enduring belief in the crucial role parents play in their children's learning. Since her early teaching days she has thought that working with parents holds an important key to the learning dispositions of their children and that if parental confidence and self-esteem are developed this has enormous benefits, for families, children and the community. She has therefore been determined to ensure that parents have access to the Centre is as many ways as possible and receive the support and education they need through a variety of means and agencies (manager interview 2).

The Centre plays 'a central part in their lives, sensitively meeting the developing needs of children and adults' for many families (Ofsted, 2000). The report praises its work with parents as 'a major strength' and suggests that the 'wide variety of opportunities for meetings and discussions provided forms the core of the Centre's integrated approach'. Staff have an important role in engaging parents and are expected to work hard to get to know them so that they feel comfortable about coming into the Centre. Staff are also expected to enable parents to be interested in and engaged in their children's learning at home. This personal approach is preferred to holding parents' evenings or distributing newsletters (manager interview 1). Parents are encouraged to attend any of the many courses and support groups and be involved with their children's welfare and education as closely as possible. As well as workshops and courses, parents have access to the parent and baby group, parent and toddler group, toy library, crèche support, outreach workers, and extended day care provision. Many meetings, courses and coffee mornings are organised around topical issues, with parents invited to ask questions, raise issues and offer suggestions.

The community medical officer and health visitor hold weekly meetings at the Centre as well as monthly clinics. Parents are able to access these services and discuss health issues, and, according to Ofsted, 'find it most helpful to have concerns dealt with quickly and informally.' Centre staff will also accompany parents to their GP or provide child care while parents receive advice from other professionals (Ofsted, 2000).

Links with specialist agencies, especially a National Children's Homes Project, enables the Centre to access further family support and parent counselling where necessary and Ofsted notes that, together, these two institutions provide a 'very comprehensive range of assessment, therapy and support services'. The Centre provides facilities for access visits for parents living apart from their children (Ofsted, 2000). It also has a caravan on the coast which parents can book for a nominal rent (note on observation).

There is a genuine desire amongst staff to work in close partnership with parents over their children's learning. Besides receiving information informally, on a daily basis if necessary, parents may discuss their child's progress on a one-to-one basis with staff members in individually arranged meetings. At these times the Record of Achievement provides the focus for discussion and parents can have this meeting at the Centre or at home if they prefer (manager interview 1). Parents and key workers are encouraged to talk about their children so that a particular approach taken by a parent over an issue, e.g. the death of a family pet, can be responded to similarly by the key worker (parental interview 1).

The Centre encourages joint learning at home by inviting parents to use the toy library (parent interview 4). The library is stocked with quality educational toys and games that would generally be too expensive for most parents (research observations).

Parents are highly satisfied with what the Centre provides for them and their children. They appreciate the staff for their approachability and genuine care and interest in their children. The key worker system is praised, not only as an effective way of providing continuity and monitoring progress, but also for providing parents with a named person with whom to communicate directly whatever the issue. One parent is impressed by seeing the policies put into practice rather than just written down (parent interview 2). There seems to be a general consensus that the Centre has changed their lives in a variety of positive ways, for example finding a new job, going to college, or having time to oneself. Several parents express particular gratitude for the non-judgmental support received through difficult personal times (parent interviews).

In addition to meetings and courses organised on a wide range of issues there is a drive to improve the general health of the community. Many sessions are jointly organised and led by a number of agencies and it is evident that health issues (in a holistic sense) have a high profile. These few examples offer a flavour of the range – a 'Keeping Safe' programme, PALS in Pregnancy, dental and oral hygiene and provision of healthy snacks (assessment of integrated work document).

Ofsted reports that parents speak highly of the adult education opportunities made available to them and identify confidence building as a key outcome. For some this has led to employment, for others potential work as childminders, and for others entry into further and higher education (Ofsted, 2000). This fits in well with the aims of the Governments Early Excellence Programme.

The atmosphere and ethos

The Centre aims to extend to parents, children and visitors a welcome which is accepting and non-judgmental. Parents are free to stay when and for as long as they like. The unit is a happy, busy, safe and secure environment. The surroundings are bright, with children's work and photographs displayed. Children appear happy and confident (field notes).

The Centre tries to ensure a high level of security and familiarity by organising the children to work within key worker groups who are responsible for their day-to-day care. This is enhanced further by the policy of moving key workers up from the 2-3+ unit to the 3-4+ unit with their children, which provides opportunities for close, uninterrupted attention over two years. This arrangement develops greater intimacy between key workers and parents as well as the children, and key workers are viewed by the majority of parents as supportive friends.

The children work in a climate where they are valued and respected (parent interviews) and where the principles of equal opportunities are upheld. Racial and cultural differences are celebrated and discrimination is not apparent from either children or adults. Staff also model high personal, social and behavioural standards which are reflected in the behaviour of the majority of the children (field notes).

Special needs

Ofsted reports that children with special educational needs (SEN) 'are very well supported and appropriately included, as are parents and carers'. It notes that the children make 'good progress' and have their individual needs carefully assessed and planned for with work well matched to their needs and capabilities. Children who are learning English as an additional language (EAL) also make good progress and the report comments on the positive presence of a bilingual member of staff (Ofsted, 2000).

The Centre believes that 'children with Special Educational Needs have a right to the same quality educational opportunities as their peers' and that 'inclusive education from birth enhances the provision for all'. It aims to achieve these aims and provide multi-agency support and early identification and intervention by employing the necessary staff. A full time SENCO deals with the administration and offers support to others in writing and delivering Individual Education Plans (IEPs). A full-time Nursery Officer is also employed to support the SENCO and two part time LSAs to work with individual children. A Portage Worker (funded by Social Services to work with families of children with special needs) also works in the homes of individual families as part of an early intervention programme (induction booklet).

The unit benefits from funding to support home language and EAL, through the employment of the EMAG teacher and bilingual assistants. Children with speech problems or delay are seen by a speech therapist who attends for two half days each week.

The key worker system and daily team meetings provides a conduit for regular information exchange between all team members and Learning Support Assistants are encouraged to contribute on the progress of their children.

Staff co-operation

Co-operation between staff seems to function at a fairly high level. The Centre is well managed, with a clear philosophy, supportive policies and procedures in place and with many opportunities for staff to make themselves heard in regular team and staff meetings. An ethos of equality and collegiality is likely to be nurtured within the Centre where systems exist to encourage professional development in real terms and where there is an 'unwritten ethos of building on individual strengths' (manager interview 1). However the hierarchical structure that manages this complex system may well inhibit levels of collegiality and joint decision making.

From conversations with various unit staff it can be deduced that the unit has had a recent history of identifying and improving collaboration with the current coordinator, who is a long serving member of staff and well respected, together with some organisational changes, e.g. the use of learning zones (field notes). There are some indications that members of staff who lack qualifications have been identified for extra training and support.

Pedagogy

Children access the curriculum through adult-led and adult-initiated activities planned according to the Early Learning Goals. These plans are determined from long term plans and children's individual needs identified through on-going observations. Well-established routines are in place that cater for individuals, pair and small group work and also for larger groups supported or led by adults (observations). In addition the children are encouraged to determine and pursue their own experiences by choosing the equipment and materials they need which are organised for easy access. Independence and autonomy is encouraged and effort is made to create a 'home' environment where the children feel comfortable and therefore confident enough to pursue their personal interests (nursery teacher interview).

The unit co-ordinator insists that good practice develops from the quality of interactions with the children that are based on a deep level of respect that arises from acknowledging the extent and depth of their emotional state at any one time (nursery teacher interview). The policy states that adults should take every opportunity to extend children's language and literacy and develop a positive attitude to communicating by listening actively and responding accordingly (policy document). Observations show that the quality of interactions is good, with adults able to extend understanding by skilful use of a variety of questioning techniques. Adults frequently participate and/or intervene to extend imaginative play (observations). The high level of staffing allows for many opportunities for interactions to occur.

The role of staff in relation to the children is, if working in accordance to the philosophy of the co-ordinator, one which responds imaginatively and with full engagement to children while they pursue their own lines of exploration and investigation. They are also expected to make regular assessments through close observation of the child's activities.

Staff are expected to enable parents to be interested in and engage in their children's learning. They do this by encouraging parents to stay, and by making them feel welcome when they do. They are expected to be sensitive to parents' needs, both individually and collectively and respond accordingly. This can entail referring to other members of staff or particular agencies or identifying areas for future workshops or courses (manager interview, field notes).

Continuity and progression in learning is ensured by regular observations of children, the results of which are entered into individual Records of Achievement. Information is collected from the initial home visit and through the settling in period. Comments are entered in relation to an area of learning every few days and significant drawings, photos and written pieces of work are added to form a comprehensive dossier from which the Pupil Profiles are written to be sent on to the primary classes. The Records of Achievement are given to the parents when the child leaves. However, parents are involved in discussions with key workers about their child's progress on a regular basis.

2

Integrating children's services: the case for child protection

Margaret McCullough

Introduction

Throughout the UK, provision and means of delivering children's services have been changing profoundly. Predominant among the reasons driving these changes is concern about the way in which children are kept safe.

The report of Lord Laming's inquiry into the death of 8-year-old Victoria Climbié, published in 2003, the commissioned report of the Joint Inspectors of Services, entitled *Safeguarding Children*, published in the same year, along with the Labour Government's pledge to combat child poverty, together have led to substantive changes in the way that all services for children are being delivered in the UK. The primary goal was identified as needing to make services better integrated in order to promote improved communication between agencies. England, Wales and Northern Ireland have each determined their own ways of implementing these changes. In 2002 the Scottish Executive published the findings of its own inquiry into child protection processes, which had been prompted by the murder of another child, three-year-old Kennedy McFarlane (Daniel, 2004). The findings reflected remarkably similar issues to those identified by both Lord Laming and the Joint Chief Inspectors of Services.

The government has issued basic guidelines regarding how children's services should be developed and integrated, but allows individual local authorities to work out its own means of interpreting them. A number of 'pathfinding' or 'trail-blazing' local authorities were identified to lead the way in initiating the radical changes the government is seeking. The remaining authorities have moved in the same direction, but at a somewhat slower pace, drawing from the experience of the 'pathfinders'. The Government has required all local authorities to have in place a Children's Trust, that is, a multi-agency governing body, by 2008.

This chapter looks specifically at how child protection services in England are being included in this process. It draws from the case studies of two local authorities, one of which is a 'pathfinder'. How these local authorities have approached the integration of services for children is considered, with particular reference to how child protection services are viewed and incorporated within the process of integration. Evidence is drawn from interviews with professionals closely involved with child protection work in both local authorities.

The chapter begins by mapping out the background to the recent developments and exploring some of the key documents and initiatives introduced by the government, before moving on to looking at how these innovations have been received by practitioners and implemented by managers, and the progress that is being made on the ground.

The background to the integration of children's services

Eight-year-old Victoria Climbié came to the UK to receive a good education and to be cared for by her great-aunt, Marie Therese Kouao. Instead, after just ten months in England, Victoria was brutally murdered by Kouao and her partner, Karl Manning. The appalling treatment to which they subjected Victoria was poignantly and extensively documented in a report that followed a full inquiry into her death led by Lord Laming. Victoria never went to school in England, but she was known to several different agencies, none of who picked up on the abusive treatment she was suffering. In Laming's detailed and damning report, twelve different occasions were identified when appropriate intervention by one or more of these agencies could have saved Victoria's life (Laming, 2003, p4). In his summing up, Lord Laming noted that 'the legislative framework for protecting children is basically sound. I conclude that the gap is not a matter of law but in its implementation' (*ibid*, p7). Tragically, Victoria's name was to join the apparently endless list of children whose deaths were attributed indirectly to poor communication between agencies that could and should have provided protection. Lord Laming made an astounding 108 recommendations for consideration by central government as well as at the individual agencies that had had contact with Victoria.

Lord Laming's report into Victoria's death was published at much the same time as the Joint Chief Inspectors of Services produced their report, which looked in considerable detail at the way in which child protection services were provided across all relevant agencies. Their report, *Safeguarding Children*, had been commissioned by the Government in 1998, and made many observations similar to those of Lord Laming about the shortcomings of the existing services. It put forward suggestions and recommendations that echoed those of Lord Laming, in relation to joint agency training, retention and recruitment of staff, and inter-agency communication (DoH, 2002).

The Government had to rise to the challenge of these powerful recommendations and consider ways of introducing the substantial changes called for in these reports in the way services are delivered to children.

The Government's agenda for change
Children's Trusts

The Government's response to Lord Laming and the Safeguarding Children report came in the form of the *Every Child Matters* Green Paper (DoH, 2004, p.4). A central plank of this document, and the Children Act 2004 which enshrines it in law, is the requirement for local authorities to bring together their services for children from the top down, in the form of Children's Trusts.

In 2003 thirty-five local authorities in England were identified as 'pathfinders' and they set to work immediately, setting up Children's Trusts and redesigning their services in ways that best suited the needs of their local population (University of East Anglia and National Children's Bureau, 2005, p1). Most of the remaining local authorities in England have now brought together the heretofore discrete roles of Director of Social Services and Director of Education, creating the new post of 'Director of Children's Services'.

Sure Start

It is not only through Children's Trusts, however, that changes to children's services have begun to emerge. In the context of their promise to eradicate child poverty by 2020, the Government has committed a large sum of money to the development of a range of children's services under the auspices of Sure Start, an agency set up by the government for this purpose. Sure Start has been charged with the responsibility of overseeing the development of new services for children as well as expanding the number of childcare places. One manifestation of these new joined-up services is children's centres, as described by Tunstill *et al* (2005 p167):

> Children's Centres are seen as key agencies in joining-up a wide range of services spanning childcare, pre-school, family support, health, employment guidance and training.

The DfES *Five Year Strategy for Children and Learners* (DfES, 2004a) drew upon the evidence emerging from Sylva *et al*'s 2003 *Effective Provision of Pre-school Education* (EPPE) study (Tunstill *et al*, 2005, p.166). It sets out the type of services that it is envisaged children's centres should deliver: a centre where health and employment advice could be accessed alongside good quality childcare, early years education and family support, all under one roof. Such centres would be located in the heart of communities, within easy reach of the local population.

The government, however, also wanted to highlight the importance of safe-guarding children in the development of universal services:

> The development of children's centres should help improve the quality of life for all children. Social workers and social care workers working with other agencies will have an important role in supporting universal services in meeting a wider range of needs. ... The duty on agencies to safeguard and promote children's welfare, Section 11 of the Children Act 2004, should help ensure safeguarding and promoting children's welfare becomes everyone's business. (DoH, 2004b, p3-4)

Safeguarding children

The *National Service Framework for Children, Young People and Maternity Services* sets out the government's vision for child protection services. Standard 5 of the document states:

> All agencies work to prevent children suffering harm and to promote their welfare, provide them with the services they require to address their identified needs, and safeguard children who are being, or who are likely to be, harmed. (DoH, 2004a, p17)

This indisputably sets out the Government's goal to engage all services in the drive towards better safeguarding of children largely through prevention. It renders integrated working essential and shifts the focus away from Social Services as the predominant provider in child protection (Payne, 2005). The role of social workers, set out in *Every Child Matters: Change for Children in Social Care*, is broadened into one of '... trying to improve outcomes for the most vulnerable...including those in need of protection...' (DfES, 2004b, p2). Corby (2006, p71) highlights the rather anomalous fact that safeguarding children is not central either to the Green Paper or to the Children Act 2004, in spite of the significant concerns identified in Lord Laming's report. It would appear that existing responsibilities in terms of investigation of serious concerns about a child's safety and welfare, deciding on the need to call child protection case conferences, and applying for court orders will remain the domain of social workers. The issue of training is further evidence of this trend. The training referred to in *Every Child Matters: Change for Children* (DoH, 2004b) includes, largely by implication, training in child protection, but this is not addressed explicitly. Indeed, this is the tone of the whole document. Safeguarding children is generally referred to in terms of prevention rather than intervention. Indeed, Corby (2006) suggests that 'the whole thrust of... *Every Child Matters...* is preventative' (p213). This represents a significant shift in emphasis in terms of early years and social work practice.

Prevention rather than intervention

The debate around prevention versus intervention has gone on for generations (Corby, 2006, p242). During the1990s there has been a growing trend towards the approach of supporting families in a preventative manner and away from more direct intervention in families where abuse has occurred or is likely to occur. The Government has now come down firmly in favour of prevention as the way forward:

> The way that services are delivered will change radically as they become integrated around the child or young person and their family and carers. There will be increased emphasis on early identification and earlier intervention. (DoH, 2005, p3)

By injecting large amounts of money into providing early years services, through Sure Start initiatives, initially in the country's 20% most deprived areas, the Government is making a two-pronged attack: first in relation to assisting children in achieving better outcomes in their education and later lives, but secondly, with regard to recognising that very significant numbers of families in contact with the child care services have multiple difficulties and disadvantages, including poverty, disorganised neighbourhoods, substance abuse and domestic violence (Corby, 2006). There is an implicit hope that by providing good quality care and support for children and families, particularly amongst the most disadvantaged sectors of society, there will be reduced levels of child abuse, as well as higher levels of achievement in school and beyond. The focus now is on universal services, that is to say facilities that are available and accessible to all.

However, the Government has also recognised that there remains a need for additional specialist services and 'targeted services for specific groups' (DoH,

2003, p4). While this does not specifically identify families in which abuse has been identified, or where there is significant risk of its occurrence, the implication is that these families will be one of these 'specific groups'. How well these services can be integrated will be addressed later in this chapter

Joint Training

Staff training was highlighted in both Lord Laming's and the Joint Chief Inspector's reports. Once again they speak as one voice in their recognition of the importance of staff receiving joint training. One of *Safeguarding Children's* recommendations identifies the importance of ensuring that

> There is a an appropriate range and quantity of joint and single agency training to meet the needs of the workforce of constituent agencies. (DoH, 2002, p9)

Prior to 2004, Area Child Protection Committees (ACPCs), multi-agency committees set up to oversee local child protection processes, had a responsibility (though not a statutory one) for ensuring adequate training on child protection was provided to staff from all disciplines. ACPCs have now been replaced by Local Safeguarding Children Boards (LSCBs), which have been given statutory duties under the Children Act 2004. One of these relates to staff training:

> It is the responsibility of the LSCB to ensure that single agency and inter-agency training on safeguarding and promoting welfare is provided in order to meet local needs. (DoH, 2006, p51)

This provides further evidence, if needed, of the Government's commitment to ensure that powers, duties and responsibilities regarding the safeguarding of children are clearly identified and enshrined in law. The issue of joint training has also been taken up by the pathfinding Children's Trusts. The 2005 National Evaluation of Children's Trusts confirms that most of the pathfinders reported that they had made arrangements 'for multi-disciplinary and inter-agency training for members of the child and family workforce' (UEA/NCB, 2005, p4). Not all of this would be specifically around child protection, of course, but much of it would have a bearing on it, for example, training on other new initiatives such as the Common Assessment Framework, the Information Sharing Index and the Information Sharing and Assessment.

These latter initiatives are likely to be the golden thread that runs through all agencies and introduces an element of enforced collaboration. The Common Assessment Framework was set out in *Every Child Matters: Change for Children* (DoH, 2004) as a means of averting crises in families through early detection and intervention. Having completed its piloting process, it was introduced across the country in April 2006 with the expectation that it will be fully embedded by 2008. Its aims included:

- Providing a method of assessment to support earlier intervention
- Improving joint working and communication between practitioners by embedding a common language of assessment and need
- Improving co-ordination and consistency between assessments, leading to fewer and shorter specialist assessments
- Enabling a picture of a child to be built up over time and shared among professionals (with consent)

It was also hoped that it would reduce the stress on families needing services by no longer requiring them to repeat information over and over to different professionals. There was a further goal that it would close gaps and loopholes between services, through which children have so easily fallen, sometimes with catastrophic results, as for Victoria Climbié. Child protection teams would necessarily be part of such a process.

The Information Sharing Index is an electronic means of storing and sharing basic information about a child. Following a pilot where different models were tested by trailblazer local authorities, the government has decided that the index should contain a central index of information about children, which is partitioned into 150 parts, one part for each local authority. The local authorities are responsible for maintaining the accuracy of their part. The government has committed itself to a national rollout by the end of 2008 (HM Government, 2006, p1).

This massive electronic database,

> will allow practitioners to identify and to contact one another easily and quickly to share relevant information about children who need services or about whom they have welfare concerns. (Miller, 2006, p14)

These new processes are clearly designed to respond directly to the failings of the system, identified by Lord Laming, which let Victoria Climbié down so tragically. They also require a substantial level of inter-agency communication in their implementation, thereby leading (or pushing) agencies to work in a more collaborative manner. The government has also pledged that it will provide funding for training to ensure these new systems are fully embedded and utilised in practice (DfES, 2005).

Closely linked to this is the Information Sharing and Assessment (ISA) initiative that also reflects the government's concern about issues of inter-agency communication. The ISA provides guidance to professionals on how they should communicate with other agencies about the needs of a child, understanding what information should be shared, with whom and under what circumstances, as well as the dangers of not doing so (DfES, 2006, p1). Within this is an explicit recognition 'that it is the changes in culture, organisation and practices that are key to success' (DfES, 2005. p1).

The Case Studies

The two local authorities I have chosen to focus on have some strong similarities, but also many differences in terms of their population and demography. Of particular importance here is that both have areas within them that have been identified by government as being amongst the 20% most disadvantaged in the country, so that each has a significant Sure Start presence in some areas at least. Other comparisons do not have a direct bearing on the issues under discussion here.

The first local authority case study was identified in 2000 as a trailblazer in the development of Sure Start's local programmes. 'Timton', as it will be called, was one of the eleven local authorities that were called upon to be path-finders in the development of the Information Sharing and Assessment system. Interviews were undertaken with a Sure Start outreach co-ordinator and a local authority Children's Safeguarding Team manager.

In contrast, the second local authority (to be referred to as 'Longton') began its move towards developing integrated services much later than Timton. In January 2006 the newly appointed Director of Children's Services in Longton put in place the first tier of management of the Directorate. Practitioners interviewed for this study were unclear also about how services would be developed and integrated. A Family Centre Manager and an Assistant Manager of a Children and Families Team from this local authority were interviewed.

Perhaps the most significant contrast between the two local authorities was the perception of integrated working. The outreach co-ordinator with Sure Start in Timton had been heavily involved in the development of Sure Start services since its inception and had invested much time forging and maintaining relationships with other professionals, devising service level agreements with partner agencies, and establishing services in sometimes virgin territory within the area, where none previously existed. This work was facilitated by a clear commitment to Sure Start and its aims within the highest echelons of the local authority. Support at this level reflects Darlington *et al*'s (2005, p246) research, which emphasises

> ...the need for decision-makers...to match current rhetoric about the need for collaboration with resources in the form of staff training and time to make this possible.

After six years the benefits are self-evident. Close working relationships and many new and innovative ideas involving a range of professionals were described to me. One example is the services for new and expectant mothers:

> Midwives have been appointed to work with Sure Start through a Service Level Agreement. They refer all newly pregnant women to us (the outreach team) at three months gestation and will let us know if there are particular needs they might have (this might be housing or financial difficulties, health issues, substance misuse or child protection concerns). We visit them when they are five months pregnant, or earlier if necessary, and tell them about the services Sure Start has to offer and the support the outreach team can give them. If they don't want to take these up at that time we will contact them again at 32 weeks gestation and again two months after the baby is born.
>
> These women can be seen by midwives for their ante-natal checks at our baby cafés and at home, which means they don't have to go to a GP surgery or hospital, which are often quite far away with inadequate public transport to enable them to get there. After the baby's birth, they can continue to go to the baby cafés where they can socialise with other parents. They can have their babies' weight checked by members of the Sure Start Community Involvement Team, who have been specially trained to do so by health visitors in the area. The health visitors also run their postnatal clinics at the baby cafés.

The co-ordination and interagency links described here surely illustrate the kind of collaboration that Sanders (2004) identifies as helping to reduce gaps between services, and Wigfall and Moss (2001, p71) see as giving 'easier access to general and specialist services, addressing all of their family's needs'.

The contrast with Longton could hardly be starker. An assistant team manager of a child protection team talked about the absence of a culture of integrated working. I was told of teams working quite independently of one another, even within social services. In place of collaboration what was described to me was a sense of dependency on the child protection team. All agencies and other social services teams refer all concerns about child protection, however small, to the child protection team. 'Other agencies won't take any ownership' was how it was explained. Child protection social workers, therefore, constantly feel under tremendous pressure, undertaking assessments that colleagues from other teams could probably have managed to carry out quite successfully. The cloud hanging over the team was the dread that they might 'miss a real cause for concern' because of their preoccupation with so many less serious cases. The case of Victoria Climbié and her social worker, Lisa Arthurworry, casts a long shadow.

Some of the referrals received by the child protection team were of cases already being well catered for by other teams and the role the child protection team could play was questionable, as in this case:

> A young single mother with two young children was receiving support from the Family Assessment and Support Team (FAST). Concerns about the mother grew when she began to express her thoughts about wanting to walk out on the children when she felt under stress. The case was referred to the child protection team who found, on exploration of the family's circumstances, that this mother was already receiving support from the teenage pregnancy service, the housing department, Sure Start, the health visitor and the GP. 'I don't know what we were expected to be able to add', the assistant team manager told me.

The support systems are evidently available; what appears to be lacking is joint working practices between these agencies. This mother was clearly well supported, but the anxiety about potential harm to the children could not be 'held' by the workers involved and had to be passed on to the child protection team, apparently more as a protective measure for the workers than for the children concerned. Had the workers been working more collaboratively, the interviewee believed that they could have managed the anxiety more effectively.

This approach is wholly consistent with that identified within the Scottish system explored in Daniel's (2004) research, following the inquiry into the death of Kennedy McFarlane. She describes a process in which children are 'referred (by health and education) *into* a child protection system, rather than being integral to the protective system' (p255). Daniel goes on to suggest that the referral carries with it the implicit handing over of responsibility for the child's well-being and future decision-making regarding intervention. The Scottish system, mirrored in Longton, allows professionals to see child protection 'as an activity carried out by social services and the police' (Daniel, 2004, p255), and not as their responsibility.

Such difficulties were not unfamiliar in Timton, although these had largely been eradicated. The Safeguarding Team manager put it down to their clear thresholds for accepting referrals, which are closely adhered to. As time goes on, growing numbers of professionals from other agencies are accepting their responsibilities for protecting children and acting on advice from the Safeguarding Team's Helpdesk, which can be called upon for advice and guidance. This is not always successful, however, and not all professionals are ready to take on the management of risky situations. While this tended to be commonplace in the first years of the recent changes, they are becoming far less so because of the ongoing work being provided by the Safeguarding Team to help professionals to manage their anxieties and bear the risk which Social Services has had to assume up till now. The Safeguarding Team manager readily acknowledges the difficulty other professionals have in taking on these responsibilities and expressed a real willingness to share the skills that social workers have developed to enable and empower their colleagues to cope with risky situations. The metaphor of 'holding the baton' has been used in Timton to help professionals understand the notion of taking responsibility in cases where there is concern for a child.

Holding the Baton

The professional or agency that is managing the concern holds the baton (of responsibility) and ensures that what ever needs to be done is done for that child, e.g. arranging a Team Around the Child (TAC) meeting (explained below), liaising with other professionals, making referrals for additional services etc. Only when the responsibility needs to be passed on to another agency, for example the safeguarding children's team because the grounds for concern have grown and the case meets the referral criteria, is the baton passed on. The safeguarding children team holds on to the baton until they have completed their input, then they in turn will pass the baton to another professional, or possibly back to the referring agency.

This is a way of ensuring that responsibility for the safeguarding of the child is never 'dropped' or lost sight of. Only when the risk to the child is no longer evident, and the concerns have abated to the satisfaction of the professionals involved, can the baton for this child be safely put down.

The experience of integrated working in Longton in many cases seemed to rely on individual professional relationships. Both the assistant team manager and the family centre manager described cases where joint work was undertaken because of personal links between staff from different teams. The family centre manager in this local authority suggested that joint working was 'often down to good will'. A good example of a case involving the family centre and the child protection teams where good collaborative practice occurred was as follows:

Three young children were removed from their parent because of severe neglect. Efforts were being made to return the children to their parents, who had then separated. The father, a heroin addict who was managing his habit and receiving support, was to be allowed to care for the older child. The younger children were to be returned to the care of the mother. To begin with supervised contact sessions between parents and children were offered at the family centre. Both parents and workers saw this as stigmatising and unhelpful. It was agreed that the parents would join the 'stay and play' sessions run for all parents at the family centre. The family centre staff developed a good relationship with the parents and it was felt that they should undertake the parenting assessment. Links with the substance misuse team were also made (because the social worker involved had worked for that team herself at one time) to provide specialised support, with close liaison between the workers.

The National Evaluation of Children's Trusts (UEA/NCB, 2004, p.5) obtained data indicating that

Integration of service delivery, and improved collaboration between different professional groups was felt to be facilitated by joint training of staff, maintenance of a stable workforce, commitment to integration at all levels and a history of joint working.

What is concerning for Longton is the unevenness of joint working, both currently and historically. At the coalface at least, there is a feeling of patchiness, that individuals have a commitment to working jointly with colleagues from other agencies, and there is plenty of anecdotal evidence of this kind of good practice. But there is an apparent absence, from the perspective of the practitioners to whom I spoke, of any real commitment from higher management.

Both the practitioners I interviewed from Longton felt disquiet about how joint or collaborative working would evolve in the future. Both workers' roles engaged them almost exclusively in child protection work and both expressed concerns about how this part of the service would be integrated with other services for children.

The family centre manager was aware that, with the emergence of children's centres in the same locality, universal services, some of which are currently offered in the family centre, such as parenting groups, 'stay and play' and other group and childcare services, would be delivered by the new centres. The more specialised services around child protection, including assessment and more focused group work, would be retained by the family centre. A child attending a children's centre who was considered to be at risk would be referred, with their family, to the family centre to receive its specialist support. It is difficult to see where integrated working fits into such a framework.

The Longton practitioners expressed uncertainty about what their senior management's interpretation was of the Government's definition of safeguarding children, as set out in the response document to Lord Laming's report 'Keeping Children Safe' and how it would be applied in practice:

> Where there are concerns about children and young people's welfare, all agencies take all appropriate actions to address those concerns, working to agreed local policies and procedures in full partnership with local authorities. (DfES, DoH, Home Office, 2003 p1)

Whilst wider provision of universal services is emerging, the manner of 'taking appropriate action to address concerns (about children's welfare)' seems still to amount to the passing on of these concerns to another agency or team to be responded to and dealt with. The gap between universal service providers in the form of children's centres and the child protection team is clearly illustrated by the assistant team manager's comment that 'children's centres make no difference (to our work). I have no idea how many are open yet'. It was made abundantly clear that, for the moment at least, children's centre services are seen as entirely separate from the work and concerns of the child protection team.

In contrast, Timton to a large extent combines its universal and specialist services. A children's centre or baby café is available to all parents in the locality. Support through the outreach team is available to all families, and is designed as a preventative strategy. Timton does not have separate Family Centres.

In Timton the team taking these initial referrals is known as the Safeguarding Team. Sure Start staff considers families they are working with who are giving cause for concern and decide if referral to the safeguarding team is appropriate. If a referral ensues, it is assessed by social workers from the safeguarding team in the usual way. The links between the Sure Start children's centres and outreach teams, and the Safeguarding Team are well established and allow for important joint work to be undertaken. One such case was that of a child whose name was already on the child protection register:

The child had been accommodated with a relative because of substantial levels of domestic violence between the child's parents. The child's mother became pregnant and an antenatal child protection assessment was carried out.

A period of intensive work followed, led by the allocated safeguarding team social worker but involving the Sure Start outreach team (which had been involved previously when the couple's older child was at home), social services support workers and the health visitor. A programme of daily visiting was devised with all agencies involved. In addition the family attended a parenting course at the CAMHS (Child and Adolescent Mental Health) clinic as well as Sure Start neighbourhood services. A specialist Teenage Identified Midwife cared for the mother during pregnancy and was part of the daily visiting regime, and the father attended an anger management group with the Community Mental Health Team.

The protection plan, which was exceptionally demanding for the couple, was nevertheless successful, and the older child was allowed to return home to live with his parents and new sibling.

In many respects this approach does not include anything radically new; rather it reflects what has long been understood as good practice (Birchall and Hallett, 1995). Agencies involved in child protection have had the Working Together guidelines since 1988; these were updated in 1991 and 1999 and further revised in 2006 (DfES, 2006). This guidance introduced the need for increased levels of participation of parents and greater emphasis on communication between professionals. Although poor inter-agency communication has been identified as a contributory factor in many inquiries into children's murders, including that of Victoria Climbié, there have, nevertheless, undoubtedly been many unsung examples across the country over the past twenty years of good multi-agency working to the obvious benefit of families and protection of children. What is different today is the integration of the agencies themselves, in terms of management structures and statutory requirements via Children's Trusts. The Timton safeguarding team manager spoke of an ethos that is no longer about demarcation of roles, but about sharing responsibility for children's wellbeing across agencies and professional groups. The approach of Timton is increasingly one of professionals working together towards the common goal of improving the lives of children, providing their particular expertise when needed, and taking their part in ensuring that children do not come to harm.

In Timton, the level of management support for the development of new services for children and the move towards integrated structures has, according to the outreach co-ordinator, allowed a culture of co-operation to develop. The Team Around the Child (TAC) approach is one such initiative.

The Team Around the Child

Here a professional identifies a child who may be in need of support, but is not at risk of imminent harm. This worker can call together a small group of other professionals and a plan can be drawn up mapping the way in which this child and family can be supported. The TAC team is similar to the 'core groups' set up after a child protection case conference, except that TAC teams would be involved before any abuse occurred and a social worker need not be involved.

Both professionals interviewed saw the joint agency training that was provided at an early stage as key to the increased collaboration between agencies in Timton. The safeguarding team manager described provision of 'massive training events' relating to the Team Around the Child approach, and the Common Assessment Framework, which all parts of the children's workforce were actively encouraged to attend. 'It was more or less a three-line-whip', I was informed. From the beginning, staff came together to attend training courses that both set the tone for future joint working and created opportunities for professional barriers to begin to be broken down. Recent research supports the use of training as a means of 'finding ways to encourage (professionals) to be reflexive about their own identities' and providing opportunities for 'a 'communication mindset' (to be) developed and supported (White and Featherstone, 2005, p215).

In comparison, the staff I interviewed from Longton had no knowledge of any existing or planned training relating to any aspect of multi-agency working. The PCT (NHS Primary Care Teams) did indeed offer 'a lot of multi-agency training', that is to say training offered to practitioners on a range of issues including child protection, but the family centre manager felt that in relation to multi-agency working, training, preparation and direction from senior management in the local authority was inadequate. The assistant team manager pointed out that even in early 2006 no information about training had been forthcoming from management in relation to the implementation of the Common Assessment Framework, which was due to be in place by April of that year. The question of whether management recognised the importance of issues of integration, such as culture and professional identity, was preoccupying the assistant team manager. Concern was expressed that changes would be dictated from above with little or no consultation and the consequences of inadequate preparation would have to be dealt with by workers on the ground.

Anning and Edwards (2006, p164) recognise the need for support from management in times of change:

> Policy changes at the outer, macro level of systems can seem oppressive to those struggling to implement them at the micro-level of their workplaces... practitioners need support at critical times to enable them to face up to and manage change.

Taking a rather pessimistic view, the assistant team manager expressed serious concern that the weight of responsibility for effective integrated working would fall to the practitioners at the coalface, as there was little evidence that senior management was recognising these issues of professional culture and identity surrounding collaborative working, let alone providing the opportunities and training needed to address them. The emphasis thus far seemed to be on structure, with little consultation with those delivering the services. Little (2005, p3) laments such an approach:

> Sadly most local authorities will begin with structures and then spend several years trying to fit the children, the evidence about need, the services and the ideas about outcomes into those structures. And in the worst case scenarios thinking that it will start and end with structures.

Adding further weight to this practitioner's concerns are the findings of Darlington *et al*'s (2005, p240) research, which suggests that the goodwill that exists between workers from different agencies to work collaboratively can be hindered by 'a lack of supportive structures and policies'.

More hopeful is the response of the Timton Safeguarding Team manager, who believes that, while it may take ten years for the impact of the preventative work being instituted now to bear fruit, 'outcomes for children can't but improve.' There is a confidence evident here that suggests that these new processes are valuable and valued by workers and service users alike.

Conclusion

This chapter considers how child protection services are being incorporated into the development of new integrated children's services by looking at two local authorities at different stages in the process of integration. What have emerged are several issues that seem to be integral to the achievement of real integration of child protection services within children's services generally.

First, it is interesting that although the changes the government has introduced through the Green Paper and the Children Act 2004 have been heralded as innovative and challenging, there is substantial continuity of established practice for social workers in child protection work. Collaboration has been central to their approach for many years, and the *Every Child Matters* documents do not significantly alter the way in which social workers approach and work in cases of child abuse. The new goals of integrated working are little different to what would have been judged good practice before the death of Victoria Climbié. The problem lay in the inconsistency of implementation rather than the underlying principles.

The welcome change emanating from the Green Paper, therefore, lies in the expectation, indeed legal duty, placed on all professionals and agencies to share in the responsibility for dealing with and managing child protection concerns. This raises important issues not only for the ways in which other professionals perceive and work with social workers, but also for the language and understanding that surrounds this area of work. It requires changes in culture and practice across the board, and how this is managed might well be predictive of how successful the move to fully integrated processes will be across local authorities.

This leads directly to the second significant finding of this research: the centrality of leadership in this process of change. The literature discusses the role of senior management in the implementation of government policy around integrated working practices. The case studies discussed in this chapter have illustrated contrasting approaches at the highest levels of management. What can be concluded is the overriding importance of the way in which the leaders of this process can provide their staff with a sense of ownership of, rather than alienation from, the changes they are expected to deliver.

Training has been seen playing a critical role at a number of levels, in the empowerment of practitioners on the ground. While the training may ostensibly be about the implementation of new initiatives such as the Common Assessment Framework or Information Sharing Assessment, it serves a number of other purposes at the same time. It provides staff with the knowledge base regarding the background to the new processes. This in turn creates the need for a new language surrounding the changes. In multi-disciplinary training, almost by definition, this language becomes shared amongst all the professional groups involved. In the process of such training, issues of culture and attitudes can be explored, so allowing opportunities for barriers to be broken down between different agencies. This research suggests that the provision of such training could be seen as a pre-requisite for success in the development of integrated practices. However, close attention needs to be paid to the nature of this training in order that it is not purely instrumental, but allows for exploration of the deeper issues and concerns with which professionals, in this research at least, have expressed a clear desire to engage.

Every Child Matters has brought about demands for manifold changes in practices. For local authorities selected as pathfinders or trail-blazers for the various initiatives there have been significant advantages, as indicated in this research. In the first place, the time scale in which the changes are to be delivered has been extended. Secondly, there have been additional resources provided, particularly for training. There are potential disadvantages too, of course. It is the trail-blazers' mistakes from which lessons are learned. But this hardly seems to make up for the speed with which non-trail-blazer local authorities are expected to implement new procedures and practices. The government has set very tight deadlines by which agencies are expected to have these in place. With a shorter lead-time and fewer resources, non-trail-blazers have a tough job to meet these demands. There is an obvious temptation to short-circuit the process and the neglect of issues of ownership and training in the rush to meet the deadlines may prove to be the first of many casualties in a wider change process.

This research flags up some of the underlying issues that either facilitate or act as barriers to child protection services being fully integrated into wider children's services. It shows that it is possible to achieve this aim, but alongside issues of practitioners' ownership of the process, the importance of leadership, the centrality of training, and the need for clear thresholds for referrals to child protection teams are also crucial. If social workers are to be expected to deal appropriately and effectively with acute cases of actual or suspected child abuse, they need to be given the authority to refuse those cases which can be satisfactorily dealt with elsewhere. They cannot be allowed to remain the repository for the anxieties of other professionals, which will drain limited resources and do nothing to reduce the risk of a child's tragic death. The government requires all staff working with children to take responsibility; the managers of children's services must ensure that that responsibility is shared equitably. Perhaps then child protection services can take its place as a specialist service integral to, not divorced from, the range of services available to children and their families.

Reflective Task

Review the case study of Timton and Longton. List the factors that underpin more effective inter-agency working.

References

Anning, A., and Edwards, A. (2006) *Promoting Children's Learning from Birth to Five. 2nd Edition.* Maidenhead: Oxford University Press

Birchall, E. with Hallett, C (1995) *Working Together in Child Protection.* London: HMSO

Corby, B. (2006) *Child Abuse: Towards a Knowledge Base 3rd Edition.* Maidenhead. Open University Press

Daniel, B (2004) An Overview of the Scottish Multidisciplinary Child Protection. *Review Child and Family Social Work,* 9, pp247-257

Darlington, Y., Feeney, J.A., and Rixon, K. (2005) Practice Challenges at the Intersection of Child Protection and Mental Health. *Child and Family Social Work,* 10 pp239-247

Department for Education and Skills, Department of Health and Home Office (2003) *Keeping Children Safe: the Government's Response to The Victoria Climbie Inquiry Report and Joint Chief Inspector's Report Safeguarding Children.* Cm 5861 Norwich: The Stationery Office

Department for Education and Skills (2006) *Information Sharing Practice* http//:www. DfES.gov.uk/ISA/sharing_Assessment/practice.cfm

Department for Education and Skills (2005) *Information Sharing and Assessment* http//:www.DfES.gov.uk/ISA/sharing_Assessment/intro.cfm).

Department for Education and Skills (DfES) (2004a) *Five year Strategy for Children and Learners*

Department for Education and Skills (DfES) (2004b) *Every Child Matters: Change for Children in Social Care.* London: DfES

Department of Health (DoH) (2004a) *National Service Framework for Children, Young People and Maternity Services.* London: DH Publications

Department of Health (DoH) (2004b) *Every Child Matters: Change for Children*

Department of Health (DoH) (2003) *Every Child Matters.* CM5860. London: The Stationery Office

Department of Health (DoH) (2002) *Safeguarding Children; The Joint Chief Inspectors' Report on Arrangements to Safeguard Children.* London: DH Publications

Department of Health(DoH) (1999) *Working Together to Safeguard Children*

Every Child Matters (2006) *Information sharing index: announcement* http//:www. everychildmatters.gov.uk/deliveringservices/index/announcement (accessed 19/7/06)

HM Government (2006) *Working Together to Safeguard Children* London: HMSO

Laming, Lord (2003) *The Victoria Climbié Inquiry: Report of an Inquiry by Lord Laming* CM 5730. London; The Stationery Office

Little, M (2005) *Building Effective Prevention Strategies in Children's Services*. Keynote Presentation at the National Evaluation of the Children's Fund available from http//: www.ne-cf.org. Accessed 20/7/05

Miller, A. (2006) Knowing Me, Knowing You *0-19, March 2006*

Payne, L. (2005) *Briefing – Safeguarding Children Children Now* http//:www.children now.co.uk/news 15th June 2005

Sanders, B (2004) Inter-agency and Multidisciplinary Working. Maynard, T., and Thomas, N. (2004) *An Introduction to Early Childhood Studies*. London: Sage

Sylva, K., Melhuish, E., Sammons, P., Siraj-Blatchford, I., Taggart, B., Elliot, K. (2003) *The Effective Provision of Pre-School Education (EPPE) Project: Findings from the Pre-School Period*. Research Brief No. RBX15-03. London: Department for Education and Skills

Tunstill, J., Allnock, D., Akhurst, S. and Garbers, C. (2005) Sure Start Local Programmes: Implications of Case Study Data from the National Evaluation of Sure Start *Children and Society* 19, pp158-171

University of East Anglia and National Children's Bureau (2005) *Children's Trusts: developing integrated services for children in England* http//:www.everychildmatters. gov.uk/children's-trusts/national-evaluation (Accessed Oct 2005)

Wigfall, V and Moss, P (2001) *More than the sum of its parts? A study of multi-agency childcare network*. NCB and Joseph Rowntree Foundation

White, S. and Featherstone, B. (2005) Communicating misunderstandings: multi-agency work as social practice. *Child and Family Social Work*, 10, pp.207-216

3

Multi-agency working:
the historical background

Jenny French

Integration: a new model of provision

Over the last forty years the mounting effect of global change and improved technology and communication has provided not only the greatest opportunities for learning that children have ever encountered, but also the greatest opportunity for practitioners to collate and share information. Improved information has also highlighted the large numbers of children still living in poverty and the inequitable provision of services across the country. The present government has attempted to address the issue of children living below the poverty line through policies and funding. Some successful initiatives have resulted: the development of Sure Start and Children's Centres, for example. This chapter seeks to explore the historical background against which these current policies have been set. Throughout the last forty years, there have been policies and initiatives which have foundered because of bureaucratic barriers and the intransigent methods of funding. Another barrier has been the concept of social exclusion. In the 21st Century we have an ideology that is far more socially inclusive and now, with the embedding of the *Every Child Matters* agenda (DfES, 2004) we have the opportunity to learn from past experiences and forge a new way of thinking and practice that will benefit both children and families.

Partnerships

Multi-agency working embraces two key concepts, partnership and integration, that conjure up a multitude of different definitions. Partnerships are working relationships in which different groups of people work together to support the child and family; a partnership can equally be considered to exist between a parent and a practitioner. However, building relationships with colleagues is as important as building relationships with parents. Nightingale and Payne, cited in Taylor and Woods (2005) consider the continuum of informal and more formal partnerships. They reflect on the fact that there are as many types of parenting styles as there are types of parent partnership but to them, the common factor in parent partnerships is mutual respect.

Partnership working is defined by Siraj-Blatchford (2000) as 'a working relationship that is characterised by a shared sense of purpose, mutual respect and the willingness to negotiate' (Siraj-Blatchford and Clarke, 2000, p98). So partnerships refer to all relationships forged around the child and family to ensure the educational, health and social needs of the child are met.

For partnership working to be effective service provision must be based on an integrated model in which the holistic needs of the child and family are addressed. Integrated working is not a new concept but a commonsense ideal that practitioners from each agency have managed at times to achieve. However, many have been thwarted because of the impossibility of agencies agreeing targets and being unable to transfer finance across agency boundaries.

> The key feature of an integrated service is that it acts as a service hub for the community by bringing together a range of services, usually under one roof, whose practitioners then work in a multi-agency way to deliver integrated support to children and families. (*Toolkit for managers of integrated services*, 2004)

Integrated services are not a new notion but a concept that was introduced in the 1980s to bring together fragmented service provision. This was hampered by political, professional and personal interests creating barriers that made integration and multi-agency working rarely possible until recent years.

Today, early years practitioners are expected to work within multi-agency frameworks to provide the services needed by the child and family. The agencies referred to are chiefly health, education, social services and the voluntary sector. Sadly, these agencies have traditionally provided parallel rather than complementary services for children and families, resulting in duplications in service provision, or gaps.

The pressure of change, although stressful to those involved in the process, is essential for progress. Various models of integrated practice have been developed over the years. One model in particular, at the Thomas Coram

Centre in central London, has created an integrated provision. The National Children's Bureau undertook a project to look at the changing model of provision and described 'the level of stress generated by the changes, both for the staff and users,' as being 'immense' (Wigfall and Moss, 2001). Without change, however, organisations stagnate and become complacent. Rodd (2006, p192) describes change as a people-oriented process, 'a transitional stage where learning, risk taking and creativity are required'. To achieve integration, practitioners' relationships and attitudes are not just the icing on the cake but the invaluable foundation on which effective partnerships can be successfully built.

Duffy and Marshall (chapter 6) consider not only strategic issues, but also the different operational dilemmas inherent in the provision of multi-agency working to provide cohesive services directly to the child and family. A key factor in the changing services has been the difficulty of identifying children in need: those disadvantaged through poverty, disability and social background. The working group researching differences in social class, chaired by Sir Douglas Black (DHSS, 1980) found a 'health divide' which separated those able to access services from disadvantaged families unable to access services:

> The evidence upon which the Black report was based was up-dated in 1988 in *The Health Divide* – again officially disregarded. This confirmed the Black Report's findings of significant class differences in mortality that apply at every stage (Daniel and Ivats, 1998)

1960s-1970s

The accepted family norm for the middle and working classes, which made up the vast majority of the population in post-war Britain, was summed up in the phrase, 'a woman's place is in the home'. For a mother, this meant that her life was cooking, cleaning and child rearing. Few were in full-time paid employment, although many did take on part-time, normally evening work, to supplement the earnings of the male breadwinner.

Before the 1960s, there were few modern home appliances available, and those that were available were, compared to today, very inefficient, and outside the price range of many UK households. One example of labour in the home, the weekly washing, could take at least a full day of very arduous toil. Mayall (2002) discusses the 're-analysis of the division of labour' demonstrating real changes that began in the sixties, many due to the feminist movement, particularly concerning women's legal, social, political, and economic conditions. Changing attitudes gradually ensured women's place in the labour market. However, lack of state support to provide sufficient childcare, alongside poor wages, unsociable hours and limited maternity leave did little to enhance the confidence of women.

At this time the National Health Service and Social Services, cornerstones of the Welfare State, were still comparatively in their infancy. The notion of universal provision has now become well established but we can see the foundations of present day reform already established in earlier legislation. The Welfare State introduced family allowances, child benefit and means-tested benefits that have brought about significant changes to families living in poverty. Social policy is to a large extent dominated by economic policy, because economic policy governs spending. So the sudden availability of affordable household appliances, which reduced the work load in the home, together with changing social policy, made it possible for women to opt for full time employment. However, the increasing differential between women's wages and the cost of childcare continued to prohibit many women from returning to work when their children were young.

Informal childcare became the norm, in the shape of relatives and close family friends, but it was not until the Plowden Report (CACE, 1967) that the rise in informal childcare was recognised by the Government. Matheson and Grosvenor (1999) discuss the report in terms of recognition of the need for a child-centred approach and the involvement of parents in children's education. The Plowden Report was the first piece of legislation referring to the links between social class and education, particularly primary education. The involvement of parents underpinned the initial moves towards multi-agency working in which parents would have a role. But it had taken more than twenty years to achieve these principles. Since this report, almost all other government reports have adopted the principles of communication and collaboration between teachers, agencies and parents. Nevertheless, parents living in poverty or those caring for disabled children managed with far less support than is available today.

The partnership between parents and educational workers has been described by MacNaughton (2003, p256) in terms of a conforming relationship in which the educators are the professional experts on how young children learn and, therefore, on the best ways in which children should be educated. This relationship does not value the knowledge and expertise of the parents. The professional holds the power and Carpenter *et al* (1996) state that the professionals used their position to make judgements and control what needed doing. Parent partnerships at this time did not represent a two-way exchange of views and parents were not expected to have much involvement in their children's education. Services for children were provided by different agencies and the voluntary sector offered other provision.

The growing number of mothers returning to work when their children were still young stimulated the drive for new services for all children. Moss (2005, p51) describes some of the triggers for extending the provision of childcare, which included high levels of poverty and increasing employment.

Early years provision was the domain of play groups, voluntary organisations and child minders, with the statutory sector providing for children with additional needs or requiring care. Health, education and social services were not usually located within the same geographical boundaries – they were not coterminous. This highlighted the difficulties of planning educational support for children in one geographical area when funding and services from social services or health came from somewhere else.

The statutory agencies had developed autonomous remits. Health provided services for children from 0-5, education from 5-16 and social services to adulthood. The only models of multi-agency working came from the special needs environment where provision for disabled children needed a range of differing professional inputs. Legislative changes in statutory service provision sometimes improved the outcomes for children, but often reinforced the divisions between the agencies providing services to children and their families. The gaps in provision left some children at risk of neglect and abuse.

Diagram showing the service model in which children fell through the gaps in service provision

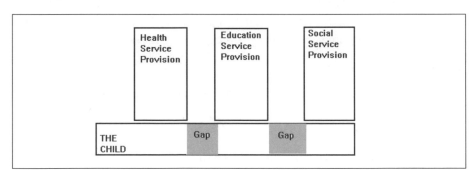

Horner (2003, p29) describes how the tragic death of a six-year-old girl had 'led to the advent of tighter managerial control of practice and the eventual establishment of inter-agency child protection systems'. Later tragedies of child neglect and death led to the implementation of the Children Act 1975 and the development of Area Child Protection Committees (ACPCs) which were the first really effective models of inter-agency working and again acted as a model for the multi-agency plans outlined by later legislation (see McCullough, chapter 2). However, each agency worked independently and provision was still fragmented.

Attempts to improve co-operation were described as collaborative or joint working initiatives. However, changing local provision to provide multi-agency working meant competing with the obstinate hierarchical determination of the managers of health, education and social services to preserve their budget allocation. They, quite naturally, wanted to retain the responsibility and funding which they viewed as their own domain. It was seen as failure if parts of services were taken over by other agencies, and often conflict arose when the funding for those services somehow could not be identified.

Play groups and nurseries worked in isolation until the play group associations provided a national framework. However, this did not include health or social services input. The recognition of the gaps in provision had begun to be identified and enlightened authorities to support multi-agency working, although this was carried out on an informal basis as there was no framework for funding to cross agency boundaries. The relevant professionals from different agencies came together to discuss the overall service provision for children. Communication between the professionals supporting the child was encouraged. In spite of these attempts, multi-agency collaboration was still impossible because of divided departmental responsibility and a split system between childcare and education. Attempts at collaborative practice were to be short lived as new social constructions emerged. Gradually political and social change developed in terms of the Rights of the Child and these changes further highlighted the gaps in provision between the services.

Summary

During the 1960s and 1970s the Welfare State continued to evolve and new ways of working had been introduced. However Health, Education and Social Service agencies had failed to work together because:

- the Welfare State was still in its infancy
- funding could not be moved between agencies
- early models of cross-agency working like the new Area Child Protection Committees were introduced
- social attitudes to disadvantage were not yet embracing the notion of an inclusive society

1980s

The 1980s heralded a significant period of change never before imagined. Britain was entering a time of greater prosperity but the poor remained poor and had limited access to services. The Conservative Government (1979-1997) implemented policy that was to change all areas of life from the service sector to the manufacturing industries, and education and social services were all reorganised to conform to the new approaches to service management. The purchaser/provider split of the late eighties brought market economics into the public sector. In health, the Area Health Authorities became purchasers who commissioned services from the providers such as family doctors. In education and social care the providers (such as day care nurseries) and purchasers (parents) had to change their working relationships as economic targets and profit and loss suddenly became an important part of a growing childcare industry.

Some parents became informed and confident, wanting to learn more about what their children were learning. However, other parents found the new emphasis on parental responsibility created a blame culture in which parents were blamed for difficulties with supporting children, and poor parenting skills. MacNaughton (2003) describes a 'conforming process' that resulted in home-school contracts being created, in which parents had to conform to the demands education made on them. Interestingly, parent partnership was a part of every piece of education legislation following the 1980 and 1981 Education Acts.

Different services provided part of the overall support children needed. Social Services provided day care and support for children in need with a range of social workers, psychotherapists and social care workers involved in the care of the child. Health provision included acute (hospital and emergency) provision and the developed community paediatric services; services like immunisation and breast-feeding advice came through family doctors. No cohesive services were developing in the national context. Siraj-Blatchford stresses the importance of the role of each professional in integrating the services provided:

> Until such times as integrated children's services are the norm, professionals must recognise that there are many factors which influence a child's development. (cited in Gammage and Meighan, 1995)

The services each produced annual Children's Plans, prioritising the needs of the children and families in their area. There was little consultation and families were expected to accept the provision recommended. Professional

Diagram showing the service model of provision in which the child and family were provided the services allocated to them

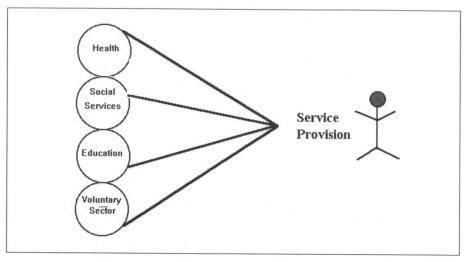

autonomy meant children could be withdrawn at the drop of a hat because the therapist or nurse had come to treat the child. After treatment the therapist rarely discussed the implication of the intervention with the teacher. There was no evaluation after treatment. Nurses and therapists felt they were visitors in school rather than part of the child's support team.

During the 1980s both social and educational inclusion required children of all backgrounds and abilities to be educated together where possible. So all those providing the services needed to understand all aspects of children's development, and also the role of other team members regardless of who the employers were. Members of each discipline had a responsibility to discuss, advise and share skills with others, although this was and continues to be hard for certain disciplines.

Triggers for changes in health came from the Black Report (1980). This report highlighted the huge discrepancy in social class take-up of services. It provided evidence of what was already widely known, that a gulf existed between families in the lower social classes and those in the middle classes.

> At birth and in the first month of life, twice as many babies of 'unskilled manual' parents (class V) die as do babies of professional class parents (class I) and in the next 11 months 4 times as many girls and 5 times as many boys. In later childhood the ratio of deaths in class V to deaths in class I falls to 1.5-2.0, (DHSS, 1980, summary point 3)

Black called this gulf the 'Health Divide', the impact of which had a lasting effect on the child's education, lifelong job opportunities and earning potential. This was later supported and re-emphasised by the Acheson Report (1998). As a result, key changes were introduced through the 1981 Education Act, the 1988 Education Reform Act and the Children Act 1989. The legislation recommended working together to protect children and to support the child.

The Children Act (1989) enabled health care staff and social workers to develop ways to work jointly in multi-disciplinary teams. Despite their valiant efforts, each agency still had different service priorities. Further difficulties arose from the economic situation in the eighties that led to service cuts and agencies retrenching. Joint working was reduced and across the area of childcare, once again, one hand did not know what the other was doing. A 'postcode lottery' of service provision developed in which children in more affluent areas accessed a greater range of services. The 1989 Children Act also promised to incorporate the principle that the best interests of the child should be paramount and that the child's views should be taken into account when making plans. Communication between the agencies, in particular the difficulty of sharing confidential information, became a barrier that has still not been effectively overcome. In some areas good working models were set up; however, this was not universal. Practitioners found themselves overwhelmed in the eighties by vast quantities of paperwork, audit and inspection that had arrived on the scene as a result of the legislation.

Difficulty existed not only in the provision of services, but at family level where needs were not heard or met. Parents were the last to be asked about the services they needed for their children. Growing waiting lists for services and childcare again meant that services for children were dependent on each agency's funding and priorities, rather than on the needs of the child. The different professionals were not co-located and parents had to take their children to different venues for assessment and then again to access services.

The climate of working together, however, was changing. Practitioners from every discipline were becoming disgruntled as the paperwork got more and more unwieldy. The adoption of 'educare' as a key approach for services for young children was introduced in England in the late 1980s. Educare became an approach which at the time changed the face of working practice. In practice, working together required a change in the ways services were commissioned. A framework for commissioning cross-agency services using Service Level Agreements (SLAs) was introduced. Local authority services and health commissioners had to work together to meet the needs of the child.

Summary

The concept of educare was introduced and a range of models of cross-agency team working developed; barriers to cross-agency working were identified. However, although an abundance of legislation had been introduced to resolve some of the issues, the fundamental foundations for multi-agency working were still not in place.

In this situation:

- funding could still not cross agency boundaries
- childcare and education remained separate provisions
- Early cross-agency commissioning caused misunderstandings and marred progress
- documents were compiled centrally by one agency so the model of cross-agency working that was advocated was not reflected centrally
- joint governance was not in place
- language barriers existed across the agencies

1990-2000

The major change that occurred in the1990s was the change from a service-driven approach to a child- and family-centred approach in provision. In a child- and family-centred approach the needs of the family triggered the services they required, as opposed to services identifying and presuming what families would need. The approach meant that the agencies would have to work together to provide the right services in the right place and at the right time for children and families.

Each new guidance and directive from the different agencies advocated many of the same key recommendations: working together, sharing skills, planning together, and targeting common issues. However, it was the 1997 Green Paper on special needs, the Education Reform Act and the 1998 SEN Programme of Action that paved the way for new collaboration. Concurrently the health recommendations from *Saving Lives: our Healthier Nation* (DOH, 1999) raised awareness of economic, environmental and social factors again and advocated working together. Phrases like 'joined-up working' were part of the New Deal from the Labour Government. The government was prepared to fund some of the major changes being advocated, now taking note of UN Rights of the Child, The Salamanca Agreement and the UNESCO Children Plans.

In 1990 the United Nations Convention on the Rights of the Child impacted on children throughout the world, giving every child the right to an identity, to freedom, to protection, and to enjoy the opportunities life offers. The convention made a significant contribution to the understanding of the individual nature of each child and the need to provide not the same universal services for all children but to tailor each provision to the needs of each child.

The first report of the UN Committee on the Rights of the Child highlighted a key issue, 'that the UK lacked an independent means to coordinate and monitor the implementation of children's rights' (Wyse, 2005). The UK was the only country in Europe at that time that did not have a Minister for Children. Wyse (2005) suggests that this, alongside other issues that were not being addressed, like corporal punishment of children, was a condemnation of government inertia. The policies which would introduce change were in place in each agency but no single government department had overall responsibility for implementation and governance.

The agencies had shifted from hierarchies to markets and networks, and words like 'streamlining', 'target-setting', 'audit trails', 'evidence-based' and 'outcomes' became introduced into agency parlance. This enabled the analysis of different issues and different interpretation of policy in each agency gradually to be addressed. The 'big three' agencies, health, education and social services, were huge, unwieldy organisations. The NHS, for example, is the largest employer in Europe; education and social services are again big employers who together had to negotiate a new working relationship to meet the requirements of the Children Act (1989). All public organisations faced a multitude of barriers, from cultural differences to different funding priorities. However, if successful, the changes would alter the way the agencies had traditionally worked and would introduce a holistic approach to childcare which would gradually become the *modus operandi* for the 21st Century.

It took until the 1990s for these initiatives gradually to influence change. Until this time both practitioners and managers providing services for children had little responsibility for reporting or monitoring their activities. They were not held responsible for their work unless, of course, their budgets were overspent. In order to implement, monitor and review change, systems had to be introduced to ensure accountability at all levels of service provision. Once again, a market economy was established within health, closely followed by social services in which a narrower purchaser/provider divide was initiated. Education was also under scrutiny, with new legislation being introduced. Organisational change, though, was longer in the making.

The role of parents

The needs of the child and family had been recognised but services were provided on the basis that the providers, rather than the users of services, knew best. New ideas were initially practice-driven, with little research evidence on which to base the changes. Initiatives like 'wrap around care' that would support working parents by offering early morning breakfast clubs and after school clubs until parents finished work and could collect their children, were being piloted. However, new ideas needed to be carefully resourced and only provided where the parents and children identified a key need for the provision. The changing role of parents was noted in the United Nations Convention on the Rights of the Child (Article 31). It was only after the School Standards and Framework Act (1998) that we saw the developing role of parent governors in schools and a value put on parents' contributions not only as support in the classroom but in the management of schools and early years settings. MacNaughton (2003) describes the transformation of the knowledge/power relationships between parents and practitioners as promoting 'democratic citizenship by inviting parents and others to form policies, manage resources and evaluate services, and by devolving decisions about what and how children should learn' (MacNaughton, 2003, p269).

Health and education services have used innovative and purposeful initiatives to address shared provision for young children. The Health Service introduced parent-held records against the backdrop of claims by providers that parents were not responsible and would lose the records. However the record was found to be valued by parents and well used by practitioners, especially health visitors (Emond, Howat, and Evans, 1995).

Confidentiality and the transfer of information about children between agencies has always been a barrier to joint working. That parents now hold records has to some extent helped to overcome the issues of confidentiality as parents can control whom they pass information to about their child. However, despite the joint planning of services at this time, discussion still frequently returned to the confidentiality issues. Social Services and Health refused to provide statistics other than anonymous aggregated figures. This impeded the joint planning process as children and families with additional needs could not be identified and service provision was *ad hoc* and delayed.

The introduction of the National Curriculum, Special Educational Needs Code of Practice, Early Learning Goals and the Foundation Stage Profile have all improved professionals' knowledge of each other's roles by moving them towards a standardisation of practice and language. Improved training of early years practitioners and the development of multi-agency planning groups and partnership committees set the foundations for the changes over the next five years. This included new opportunities for parents to train through initiatives set up by Early Years Development and Childcare Partnerships. Previously, the school had organised activities around the child and the parents were marginalised, although responsibility was left to the parents for out-of-school activities.

In spite of the many initiatives involving multi-agency working, educare had created as many tensions as it had improved working practice. Alcock (2003), discussing the improvements in health following the Black Report (1980), demonstrated that the provision of the Welfare State had apparently failed to address the inequalities between the wealthiest and the poorest people. Acheson (1998) further researched the work Black (1980) had undertaken nearly twenty years earlier and found that services for children had not reduced childhood poverty but in fact in some cases had underlined the inequalities. Many of the issues raised have now been taken up as government initiatives, especially those which affect children and young people (Taylor and Thirtle, 2005, p249).

Despite the role of the state dramatically changing, Bennet (2003) talks of the persistent division between education and care, and asserts that it is unusual for national administrations radically to rethink areas of ministerial responsibility. However, the current government found itself in a situation in which, without changes in government departments, the programmes of reform could not be implemented.

Alongside governmental changes further initiatives were needed at service level before the concept of child-centred provision could be extended. This was to become the centre of new service provision recommended in *Every Child Matters*.

The child- and family-centred model

The child- and family-centred approach is a most significant shift towards multi-agency provision and should identify whether or not services are meeting children's needs. If the service is not operating on this basic premise, questions need to address what could be improved or enhanced. This perhaps sounds naïve as resources cannot provide for every need; however, the resource argument is often an excuse for not tackling change in the first place. Participation, by way of consultation and advocacy, is a core part of the Every Child Matters initiative. Attitudes and approaches to changing policy

Diagram showing the child-centred model of provision that developed from 1990 onwards, where services were allocated according to the needs of the child and family

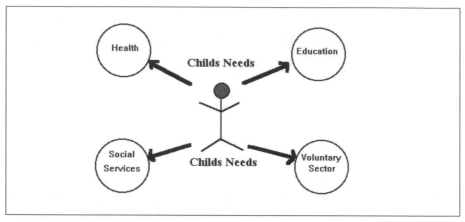

require staff to embrace new learning and so the quality and content of training has been essential in the agenda of change.

'Child-centred' means that the needs of every child are the key to the provision of services for children and their families. Child-centred approaches rely on practitioners spending time talking to children and families about what is ultimately important for them. As models of team working evolved, so did the role of the key worker who would co-ordinate the team working with the family. However, to construct a social model acceptable across agencies, child-centred provision in terms of service planning needed to be an holistic, ecological approach (Bronfenbrenner, 1979).

Pugh (1996) recognised that services in the UK were not discretionary, they varied and lacked co-ordination. The lack of an overview across agencies compounded the slow rate of change. This lack of vision highlighted the persistent division between care and education. Bennet (2003) refers to an OECD project which found that where goals such as autonomy, self esteem and socialisation were pursued, education and care were not seen as separate identities. The emphasis on change in social justice needed to be disseminated across agency boundaries, and this could only be achieved by changes in the models of team working and training in multi-agency working at all levels.

From 1996 local authorities had a mandatory duty to set out the local authority planning arrangements for children's services with annual targets and specified review arrangements. To this end the Children's Service Plans were introduced as a result of the 1989 Children Act. Jointly agreed plans were produced which went out to consultation to all partners including parents and the voluntary sector. Health no longer had a leading role in providing services for children from 0-5 years old as responsibility was shared across agencies and joint planning and commissioning emerged, with social services taking the lead in Children's Services.

Social Services were themselves re-modelling their core services as a result of the 1989 Children Act. Three new teams, Children in Need, Child Protection and Looked After Children (Horner, 2004) were set up and each of these areas required multi-agency collaboration with health and/or education. In 1992 nearly 40,000 children were on the child protection register. This number decreased and ten years later 25,700 children were on the register (see McCullough, chapter 2).

Parents were becoming much more powerful and government directives encouraged working with parents. DfEE guidance recommended that 'parents and practitioners should work together in an atmosphere of mutual respect within which children can have security and confidence' (QCA, 2000, p11).

The NHS and Social Services had primarily been set up to consider their dedicated remit of provision but also to look primarily at short term health or social problems, rather than catering for the lifelong needs of local communities. In education, teachers and practitioners would work with a group of children for one or maybe two years, again rarely thinking about the future of the child as an adult and what the long-term needs and wishes might be.

So the views of the child and family gradually became the focus of the next round of legislation. Participation, consultation and collaboration underpinned the processes leading up to the Green Paper *Every Child Matters: Change for Children* (2000). The 1989 Children Act was thought to be the best way forward for promoting collaborative approaches to childcare. However, the protection of children was to come into question again in 1999 with the death of Victoria Climbié.

The existing models, which had forced agencies to work independently, by ensuring each had individual priorities, would not change until attitudes and funding streams could meet across agency boundaries. Professional teams had to work together despite the barriers to multi-disciplinary working. Campbell (2003) highlights the difficulties and dilemmas in promoting integrated services. He includes the issues of 'shifting professional identities' in the development of early years practitioners, leading to skill sharing and 'working together'.

Some models of good practice undoubtedly existed during this time. The Thomas Coram Centre, the Pen Green Centre and many of the new Early Excellence Centres are examples. However, no changes to working practice are easily made. Wigfall and Moss (2001) published their findings on a multi-agency childcare network and summarised three constraints to multi-agency working. First, each service had its own perspective, agenda and structure and changes might have incurred a loss of service or professional identity. Secondly, time was not allocated to joint activities or training, and thirdly, the tension between the demands of providing existing services and of making multi-agency connections was seen as additional pressure on the service. These are common issues across all services.

Multi-agency working and joint working were seen as challenges to the new models being piloted through the Early Years Development and Childcare Partnerships (EYDCPs), Early Excellence Centres and the first 60 Sure Start trail-blazers.

Summary

The move has been to a situation where we see:

- child and family at the centre of provision
- consultation and participation
- models of Government departments working collaboratively
- models of good practice emerging at service level multi-agency teams
- models of multi-disciplinary team working introduced in Sure Start, EYDCP and Early Excellence Centres

2000-2006

At the beginning of the new century, early years services have come a long way. It is hard to turn the clock back to show, and celebrate, just how far we have come. Research, in the form of the EPPE (Effective Provision of Pre-school Education) has provided positive feedback on the requirements of quality provision in settings and encouraged the debate about best practice in early years. The EPPE results acknowledge that we still have a long way to go to change practice in all settings: if history has taught us one thing, it is that we cannot afford to be complacent about children's futures.

In the late 1990s the first round of Early Excellence Centres was evaluated by Bertram and Pascal (2002), who reiterated some of the issues marring multi-agency working. They address the perennial questions of the best ways to support parents and issues around good practice. Research evaluating out-comes from some of the 100 or so funded EECs (Pascal *et al*, 2002) and the on-going EPPE project (Siraj-Blatchford *et al*, 2003) have started to underpin further development of good practice. It is also possible to track changing social values and attitudes and their impact on policy for example, in terms of children's rights, especially in light of our cultural diversity. Identifying issues of inequality is key to ensuring an inclusive setting. Particular attention is now being paid to the promotion of social inclusion for isolated and dis-advantaged families, equal opportunities and race equality across all early years settings (Early Years Equality, 2006).

The new drive for children's services has come from education and this has introduced a new range of issues, this time to be addressed from a research base rather than a practice-driven base. Anning *et al* in Leeds undertook the MaTCH Project (Multi-Agency Delivery of Services to Children) which has ex-plored the processes involved in multi-agency teams delivering public and voluntary services. This project grew from a recognition that little previous research existed into ways of conceptualising and delivering new versions of services (Robinson *et al*, 2006).

Although the barriers and bonuses of multi-agency teams working are well documented, progress in improving quality provision in the new Children's Centres is reliant on teams understanding the working practices. Margaret Hodge, the first Minister for Children, stated in the introduction to the Every Child Matters agenda that better outcomes for children could be achieved by housing the services under one roof (DfES, 2004).

The new children's centres bring us up to date in this historical overview. The initial one hundred Early Excellence Centres that laid the foundations of quality in early years practice, have now become Children's Centres and are working in a range of partnerships to devolve their multi-agency skills to newly evolved teams. Strategic governance, multi-agency training initiatives and the Joint Area Reviews will continue to keep the sector abreast of progress and highlight the complexities of and constraints to joint practice.

Much research is still needed as new multi-agency working evolves. Warin (2006) asserts the need to re-conceptualise early years practice so that inte-grated services are viewed not as homogenous units but as a provision speci-fically designed to meet the needs of the child within the family. Much of the present research available reports local success stories from Sure Start pro-grammes such as the excellent joint practice described by Weinberger, Pick-stone and Hannon (2005).

Summary

This is the scenario as this book goes to press:

- *Every Child Matters* is being implemented
- parents are to be trusted and valued as partners in the provision and development of Early years Services
- provision to complement, not replace home care (EPPE)
- services for all children from birth
- Sure Start and children's centres are here to stay
- more research is needed to underpin training and practice
- the Workforce Strategy will rationalise the new model of early years practitioner and their working place beside their multi-agency team members

Conclusion

How much have we progressed over the last 46 years? One of the recommendations of the Black Report (1980) was to develop universal services, but what impact did this have on children's health? The report by Hirsch (2006) for the Joseph Rowntree Trust on ending child poverty highlighted the same fact that Acheson (1998) had revealed in his report: that little had changed so as to reduce the cycle of poverty for children and families in the UK. In some areas, the divide had even widened (Exworthy *et al*, 2003). Somehow the numerous reports have had little impact on the cycle of disadvantage and child poverty. It is remarkable how familiar this sounds when we talk about the five outcomes of the Children Act 2004. By the 1990s changes were occurring in parallel in all the main services. The wonderfully inspiring phrases 'working together', 'joined-up working', and 'reducing cross-agency boundaries' were inherent in each piece of legislation. However, as each agency was given a lead – rather than a shared – role in implementation, so the opportunity to share policy and practice disappeared into thin air.

All services for children will now be provided through jointly planned, commissioned, financed initiatives in participation and consultation with local parents. This requires a high level of integrated working across agencies, and relies on changed attitudes, the enthusiasm of practitioners, appropriate resources, and effective leadership and management. The level of commitment must be underpinned and driven by research, before training and quality of provision can be monitored and maintained over the long term. The Workforce Strategy and Common Core will help resolve issues between different professional bodies but this will take time to negotiate and implement.

People with the range of knowledge, skills, understanding and experience required are vital in meeting the needs of young children and families in the twenty-first century.

The undeniable link between poverty and unemployment and children's life-long opportunities to learn is widely researched and documented. New early years practitioners must understand that young children are the adults of tomorrow, and the importance, therefore, of breaking the persistent cycle of poverty.

References

Acheson, D (1998) *Inequalities in Health Report.* London: The Stationery Office http://www/archive.official-documents.co.uk/document/doh/ih/ih.htm

Alcock P (2003) *Social Policy in Britain, 2nd edition.* Basingstoke: Macmillan

Anning, A (2005) Investigating the impact of working in multi-agency service delivery settings, *Journal of Early Childhood Research.* 3: 19-50

Atkinson, M; Wilkin, A; Stott, A; Doherty, P and Kinder, K (2002) *Multi-agency working: a detailed study.* Slough, London: NFER

Bennett.J (2003) Starting Strong, *Journal of Early Childhood Research.* 1 (1)

Bertram T; Pascal C, Bokhari, C., Gasper, M. and Holtermann, S. (2002) *Early Excellence Centre Pilot Programme Second Evaluation Report 2000-2001*, DfES Research Report No 361, London, HMSO

Bronfenbrenner, U. (1979) *The Ecology of Human Development: Experiments by Nature and Design.* Cambridge, Mass: Harvard University Press

Campbell, A. (2003) Developing and Evaluating Early Excellence Centres in the UK: some issues in promoting integrated and 'joined-up services *International Journal of Early Years Education* Vol. 11, No. 3, October 2003

Carpenter, B. Ashdown, R. and Bovair, K. (1996) *Enabling Access; Effective Teaching and Learning for Pupils with Learning Difficulties.* London: David Fulton

Central Advisory Council for Education (CACE) (1967) *Children and their Primary Schools* (The Plowden Report) London: HMSO

Daniel, P. and Ivats, J. (1998) *Children and Social Policy.* Basingstoke: Palgrave

Department for Education and Employment (DFEE) (2000) *Curriculum Guidance for the Foundation Stage 2000.* London: Qualifications and Curriculum Authority

Department for Education and Skills (DfES 2005) *Multi-agency toolkit* www.everychildmatters.gov/deliveringservices/multiagencyworking

Department of Education and Science (DES) (1981) *Education Act.* London: HMSO

Department of Education and Skills (DfES) (2004) *Every Child Matters: Change for Children* DfES/1081/2004, Nottingham, DfES

Department for Education and Science (DfES) (2004) *Early Support Helping Every Child Succeed Background Information* Nottingham: DfES

Department of Health (DoH)(2004) *Executive Summary – National Service Framework for Children, Young People and Maternity Services.* London: DH Publications

Department of Health (DoH) (1999) *Children Act 1989 Guidance and Regulations* London: HMSO

Department of Health (DoH) (1999) *Working Together to Safeguard Children*. London: Department of Health

Department of Health (DoH) (1999) *Saving Lives: our Healthier Nation*. London: Stationery Office

Department of Health and Social Security (DHSS) (1980) *Inequalities in Health* (The Black Report) (online) http://www.sochealth.co.uk/history/black.htm

EYE (2006) *Policy for All Inequalities. Early Years Equality* (EYE) Publications

Emond, A. Howat, P. Evans, J.A. (1995) Reliability if Parent Held Child Health Records. *Health Visitor,* 68(8), 322-3

Exworthy, M., Stuart, M., Blane, D., Marmot, M (2003) *Tackling Health Inequalities Since the Acheson Inquiry*. Bristol: Policy Press

Hirsch, D. (2006) *What will it take to end child poverty?* York, Joseph Rowntree Trust.

Horner, N. (2003) *What is Social Work: Context and Perspectives.* Exeter: Learning Matters

Lave, J. and Wenger, E (2002) Legitimate peripheral participation in communities of practice. In Harrison, R. Reeve, F. Hanson, A. and Clarke, J. (2002) (Eds.) *Supporting Lifelong Learning: volume one* London: Routlege Falmer (pp. 111-126)

MacNaughton, G. (2003) *Shaping Early Childhood, Learners, Curriculum and Contexts*. Berkshire: Open University Press

Matheson, D. and Grosvenor, I. (1999) *An introduction to the study of education* London: David Fulton

Mayall, B. (2002) *Towards a Sociology for Childhood*. Buckingham: Open University Press

Moss, P. (2005) *Ethics and Politics in Early Childhood Education*. London: Routledge Falmer

Penn, H. (2001) *Early childhood services, theory, policy and practice*, Buckingham: Open University Press

Pugh, G (ed) (1996) *Contemporary Issues in the Early Years*. London: Paul Chapman Publishing

Robinson, M. Anning, A, Cottrell, D, Frost, N. and Green, J. (2006) *Service delivery through teamwork. human resources*. Public Service Review. http//:www.public service.co.uk/pub_contents.asp?id=178

Rodd, J. (2006) *Leadership in Early Childhood*. London: Open University Press

Siraj-Blatchford, I., Sylva, K., Taggart, B., Sammons, P., and Melhuish, E. (2003). *EPPE case studies Technical Paper 10*. University of London, Institute of Education/DfES

Taylor, J. and Thurtle, V. (2005) Child Health in Taylor, J. and Woods, M. (2005) *Early Childhood Studies an Holistic Introduction.(2nd Edition)* Oxford: Hodder Arnold

United Nations (1990) *World Summit for Children UN Convention on the Rights of the Child (1989)*

Warin, J. Joined up Services for young children and their Families: papering over the Cracks or re-Constructing Foundations. in *Children and Society.* (Online) Earlydoi. 1111/j.-09900860.2006.00036

Weinberger, J., Pickstone, C and Hannon, P. (2005) *Learning from Sure Start. Working with Young Children and their Families*. Maidenhead: Open University Press.

Wigfall, V. and Moss, P. (2001) *More than the sum of its parts?* London: National Children's Bureau

Wyse, D. (2005). *Childhood Studies: An Introduction.* Oxford: Blackwell

4

Keeping people in the big picture: national policy and local solutions

Martin Needham

This chapter reflects on the development of multi-agency working as a strand of national government policy and how this has influenced local policy and practice. It draws upon published research and reflection from the first ten years of the National Childcare Strategy to identify the five areas of change set out in table A (below). These five areas of change were discussed with a strategic development officer for early years services. This discussion forms a case study of a Local Authority with Beacon status for integrated service delivery, which is used to illustrate the impact national policy changes may have on local developments.

Table A: Areas of change in English government policy in relation to early years services and multi-agency working 1997- 2007

1. Change from partnership working in creating childcare places to multi-agency reform in protecting children.

2. Change from increasing economic participation in key areas to supporting families universally.

3. Change from local community involvement to greater national and local government control.

4. Change from raising educational standards by classroom reform to family support.

5. Change from increasing access to improving the quality of service provision.

Policy changes are markers of some of the key issues of national government strategy. Policy changes underline where national government is keen to effect change and, therefore, highlight areas of challenge for those developing multi-agency services.

Reflecting critically on the bigger pictures of national agendas and local needs may help multi-agency teams to develop greater understanding of the different aims and values within these communities of practice.

The case study interview, which was carried out in 2005 and updated in 2006, reflects on the process of local change. This is a process involving a move from localised areas of multi-agency working, based on Sure Start local programmes, towards increasingly widespread multi-agency working, developing multi-professional area-based teams reporting to area-based co-ordinators of children's services. The potential impact of national and local change on the cultures of communication between families and multi-agency teams is reflected upon in the following analysis.

In the case study context, multi-agency work meant developing several layers of team working around the child. These layers, likened to an onion by the local authority, echo Hugo Bronfenbrenner's ecological model (Bronfenbrenner, 1979). The concentric rings of influence in both models centre on the child and immediate family and expand out, through local group influences, through to national influences. This helps to remind us that the bigger picture does affect the child.

A change from partnership working in creating childcare places to multi-agency reform in protecting children

When elected in 1997 the New Labour Government quickly moved to initiate reform in early years and childcare services. This was in response to existing reviews of the effectiveness of early interventions from the High/Scope programme in the United States, related to the long-lasting benefits of 'high quality' early education (Schweinhart, 1993), and the success of Scandinavian early years services in helping parents return to productive employment (Ball, 1992). The creation of the National Childcare Strategy led the drive for universal early education and childcare places. In 1999 figures identifying the level of child poverty in Britain sparked a government pledge to eliminate child poverty in a generation. Local Sure Start programmes targeted populations of around 800 children aged 0-4 in some of the 20% most disadvantaged wards in England. These programmes became co-ordinators of multi-agency services, deploying unprecedented financial resources for this sector. Local programmes offered attractive community bases, communication links and some commissioning of new services in order to present a joined-up picture of services to families in targeted local areas. Nationally set targets focused on improvements in child and family health, an increased level of home support visiting and services aimed at promoting family learning, as well as childcare services that would enable parents to return to work and escape the poverty trap.

A second defining event in children's service reform was the death of Victoria Climbié in 2000 because of physical abuse and neglect. The subsequent inquiry, resulting in the Laming Report (Laming, 2003), concluded that a lack of integration between services and a lack of clear lines of accountability were major contributing factors to Victoria's death (see also McCullough, chapter 2). The government's response was the Every Child Matters strategy enacted through the Children Act 2004. This strategy sets out requirements for the establishment of single Directors of Children's Services by 2008 and for a strong push towards the development of more integrated multi-disciplinary approaches. This was coupled with workforce reforms aimed at refocusing all service providers on a shared view of children's rights related to the 'five outcomes' (safety, physical and mental health, leisure and education, citizenship, and economic well being) and the setting out of training pathways to Early Years Professional Standards (CWDC, 2006). The Common Assessment Framework (CAF) was also introduced as a forum for sharing concerns and information about children (DfES, 2006). The widening emphasis on multi-agency working is also clearly illustrated by the national policy for the creation of two to three thousand children's centres (DfES, 2004). The target to establish a children's centre supporting each parliamentary ward by 2015 established multi-agency working as major part of government policy for young children and their families, not just on a disadvantaged area basis but as increasingly universal provision for all families. It also builds on the strengths identified by research into the success of existing integrated centres and Sure Start local programmes (Sylva *et al*, 2004; Anning, 2005; Weinberger *et al*, 2005). Children's centres embody a commitment to joining up services and serving local communities and the case study analysis (overleaf) begins by reflecting on this initiative.

Here a significant change in policy is highlighted: 'joined-up thinking', which was a prominent phrase in early government policy, is moving towards more literally 'joined-up services' with health, education, and social care workers increasingly coming under a single point of management through either Children's Trusts or reshaped local authority management structures. In the

---

Case Study Interview extract 1

I think we are moving from children's centres to children's centre services. I think we need to understand what we mean by children's centre services. I think that it is a positive element to be engaging with local providers and local services, because while you might have a building it is about all those other services that feed into it, and that's where it can become a universal service. When children's centres were first discussed, talking with social care colleagues they said, well it's OK, but it's not the group of people we are dealing with. But we are trying to make sense of how all the services fit together.

We've gone away from a focus on integrated education and childcare in buildings (a requirement in initial DfES guidance) to how agencies interact with each other. You're only going to get a certain population coming into a centre. This is where we need to think about children's centre services, because how do you go out to those people who won't come in?

I suppose there is a budgetary element too: it is about this understanding about how things fit together, rather than services in the past where you had separate universal services and vulnerable children services and a huge gap in the middle, and that gap is where expensive issues start arising and intermediate issues start bubbling up and become more serious and that is what we are trying to avoid.

---

case study authority, for example, social care services for children had recently come under joint management with Education and Early Years services. These services were then linked to health and other agencies through the establishment of a Children's Trust structure that brought together senior managers from a variety of agencies into a strategic planning group. This represents a significant change for the delivery of services in the case study authority. Where those operating a centre for children in the past would have had to go to a range of different managers to access a range of professional skills, they are now likely to find those skills delivered on an area basis under a single manager or co-ordinator.

Extract 2 indicates an acknowledgment of the perceived difficulties of earlier multi-agency working where health, education and social care agencies might be working towards with different agendas and cultures. When services are perceived as being autonomous there is likely to be a prioritisation of specialised targets and competition to assume an authoritative role in particular cases. This is the pragmatic basis for creating structures where a single

---

Case Study Interview extract 2

What the Children Act means is that in all the managers' meetings the strategic people are round the table so that you are working as colleagues, which, I think, makes a big difference. The impact of it on the day-to-day operation of services probably has not had a great deal of impact yet but I think it will do. It is in the wider multi-agencies working in terms of school and community clusters, this is our way of developing the integrated services.

---

manager or board can decide on the most appropriate blend of services to be deployed in any situation. The integration of management structures was intended to offer:

- improved responsibilities and accountability (DfES, 2005 p4)
- early identification of needs (DfES, 2005 p4)
- reduced risk of children falling through gaps between services (DfES, 2005 p4)

Case Study Interview extract 3

We have moved towards a model of school and community clusters in order to have co-ordinators of co-located multi-agency teams, working in areas that aren't doing all the individual caseload support, but are making the links with other services. Training, support and advice is offered to practitioners working with families, so if somebody is a social worker it isn't necessarily that they have to go and do the job, but it might well be that they are supporting somebody else or offering support and advice. That is where we are looking at an outreach model that we developed in Sure Start local programmes. This is where we got those para-professionals with certain expertise linking through with frontline services and that is something that we are looking at even more, so that as we develop further children's centres we will be looking at that outreach model.

Extract 3 represents a practical local solution to the difficulties of delivering multi-agency working teams modelled by Sure Start local programmes but on reduced budgets, by mobilising less costly staff in preventative work and reducing management structures. A difficulty that many managers and workers may have to address is the dilution of financial resources concomitant with mainstreaming. Key professionals are likely to be shared between a number of settings and therefore in real terms the support systems for those staff in terms of record keeping and administration might also be reduced. Mainstreaming might in some cases represent a reduction in attention to the pockets of significant poverty addressed by the Sure Start local programmes.

Tunstil, reflecting on data from the National Sure Start Evaluation, notes that many studies have shown that multi-agency working introduces mixed agendas that can impede progression, highlighting the reluctance of some social workers to prioritise preventative work with families (Tunstill *et al*, 2005).

The move from semi-independent Early Years Development and Childcare Partnerships (EYDCPs) in which private, voluntary and local authority volunteer members planned for nationally prescribed targets using ring-fenced budgets, to local authority run Children's Boards, represents an acknowledgement of the failure of some agencies in some areas to respond to previous government agendas. This illustrates the lack of power experienced by many EYDCPs in focusing the attention of some agencies on young children and families, particularly where those families were not at significant risk. Interview extract 4 suggests that partnership working was perceived to have important benefits in the case study area with regard to developing effective policy that was accepted, legitimised and owned by those delivering and participating in services.

Case Study Interview extract 4

What I think has been an incredibly positive element in this authority – and I think some other authorities have lost it – is that we have maintained our Partnership (EYDCP) because those partners still feel they are signed up to something. We are reviewing it; we are looking at bringing together our two local Sure Start boards and our Partnership board as well. It isn't about control and power, but about developing respect and trust. By focusing on the family everybody feels part of it and they feel that they have to be striving.

We are very used to working to that partnership agenda. We looked at the national perspective, the Children Act, school and community clusters, children's centres, extended schools, and there is an understanding that, while we have separate things to deliver, this is the agenda we all have to work to now. We have our strategic partnerships and subgroups; they have been going for the last two years. There is more confidence because you've got those foundations. There are fears about change, but people feel secure in this partnership.

Extract 4 emphasises the importance of a forum for communication between agencies so that everyone is aware of changes, understands why teams want to move in a certain direction, and can share views about the possible implications of change to other teams. Bagely, Akerly and Rattray highlight the key importance to the success of multi-agency working of professionals being willing to work in new ways and striving to work together (Bagely *et al*, 2004). Discussing reasons for the success of a Sure Start case study, they identify the value of 'flat management structures built on mutual respect and shared problem solving' as well of the benefits of co-location for 'sharing concerns, issues and information' (Bagely *et al*, p604). Team building activities, joint strategy planning and review, joint training and professional development days can play a crucial role in facilitating understanding and shared values.

National government policy documents and associated structures such as the CAF and EYFS still emphasise partnership working; however, some professionals are now being compelled towards multi-agency working. Those developing multi-agency connections may need to strive to overcome a sense of compulsion by some partners by quickly establishing shared goals and values.

Change from increasing economic participation in key areas to supporting families universally

Several authors argue that competition in the globalising economy has been a driving force behind educational reforms (Esland, 1996). The perceived need to maximise the numbers of the available workforce and to increase the nation's human and thus economic capital, coupled with research into the potential success of early childhood interventions, has sparked interest worldwide in the early years agenda:

> There has been no major government project concerned with early childhood services *per se*, or more generally with young children as a social group, no strong agenda concerned with early childhood in its own right. Instead early childhood services and young children have become items on the agenda of two major and related projects of the new government – improving standards in school and increasing labour market participation and economic competition. (Moss, 2001, p80)

Case Study Interview extract 5 illustrates the tensions economic issues create for some professionals within the multi-disciplinary team

---

Case Study Interview extract 5

The line about getting parents back into work – it didn't feel that good. OK, you know it's a driver, but you wouldn't want that within your vision, not as explicit as that.

The ten-year childcare strategy, by having the extended maternity and paternity leave, offers increased choice. Yes, you can see that by having that choice you might not want to go back to work, but at least you feel, psychologically, you've had a choice and there's something in that. But there's the whole issue that you might get a job, but it might be very low paid and that has still got to be addressed.

If you're linking it to the economy, it's got to look beyond the children, but it can't be seen as the main driver. There is that moral bit, what do we want to happen for them to bring the children up positively.

Practitioners from many children's services have not regarded economic development as part of their role. Opinion on the importance of childcare continues to be split: for many parents and practitioners it is a vital part of personal and national economic well being, while others believe that children may be better supported by having the sustained attention of relatives in their pre-school years. At a fundamental level, families whose work prospects might encompass work with a low level of job satisfaction – whether highly paid or poorly paid – might view the push to return to work as denying them one of the most satisfying life opportunities open to them in terms of raising their children. Recent research by Leach *et al* suggests that for some children being raised with higher levels of parental care will be a great benefit (Leach *et al*, 2006); for others greater financial security and reduced exposure to stress in the home environment may offer better outcomes. This emphasises a need for flexibility in both local and national approaches, so that families are not all forced towards a stereotyped set of options (see Clarke and French, chapter 9). Flexibility was increased by extensions to maternity and paternity leave, giving parents more time to access family support services before they return to work.

A constant problem highlighted during the earlier phases of the childcare strategy was that many at risk children lived outside the identified pockets of disadvantage. The 2005 childcare strategy, children's centre agenda and Every Child Matters clearly set out the move towards universal support services. However a potential, if unintended, consequence of this shift is a distraction from tackling the underlying economic causes of poverty.

Case Study Interview extract 6

We want to get away from the Sure Start dilemma of a cut-off at the age of four. It's about looking at our resources and how we pull them together by linking extended schools and linking on school sites, keeping partners on board.

Children's centre services are offering joined-up, integrated services, but I think the big opportunity with it is making all those links with other initiatives such as what we have done within Claydale. Linking up with other initiatives, the children's centre is the starting point for regeneration in the Claydale area, linked through with other funding streams, with other partners, so that what you have now is a part of the urban regeneration and social regeneration.

Case study extract 6 highlights a view in the case study authority of multi-agency working that goes beyond the traditional boundaries of work in the field of children and families (education, social care and health) by recognising that the economic prosperity of a community has a significant bearing on the prospects of children in the area. The case study authority developed children's centre sites that included library and lifelong learning facilities to initiate training opportunities for parents. They included working units for business start up where childcare would be available on site in order to promote employment and training opportunities for local women, including community run cafés and catering opportunities. The initiative incorporated a rolling programme of visits by Job Centre Plus workers, training providers, voluntary support groups and social activities, to offer support and guidance not just to families but also to the wider community. This strategy suggests that parents are being empowered to make choices through education and training. Some parents and professionals might view these choices as still being limited and geared towards national targets rather than personal targets. The Joseph Rowntree Trust (Hirsch, 2006) highlighted that for many parents, living in poverty on benefits and caring for their children was preferable to poorly paid low-skill work opportunities when higher paid jobs remain inaccessible because of inflexible working arrangements and qualification requirements. The inclusion of neighbourhood regeneration, business and non-vocational training elements as part of a multi-disciplinary approach may help communities to take up the core elements of the 2004 Children Act. Hirsch (2006) projects that the welfare-to-work strategy will only make limited progress in the next decade in the present economic climate. The alternative Hirsch advocates is increasing benefits further and acknowledging the importance of the parenting role to a greater extent.

Change from local community involvement to greater national and local government control

Tackling poverty has been politically effective in motivating and justifying reform. Poverty, however, emphasises a view of certain communities as being disadvantaged and may to lead to feelings of otherness and alienation. In order to encourage continuing participation in services, the development of a sense of ownership and involvement has been a key aspect of successful Sure Start local programmes. The shift to universal services should serve to lessen any sense of stigma in accessing Sure Start services. However a consequence of this policy shift is that Sure Start resources will be controlled by local authorities rather than local community Sure Start boards. Norman Glass, one of the architects of Sure Start, highlighted this as a concern (Glass, 2005). This change suggests the government is relaxing targets designed to ensure community participation in partnership working. The government's apparent commitment to an ideology of local participation and ownership may be shifting to a more authoritarian stance, insisting that the government at national and local levels knows best.

Case Study Interview extract 7

From a wider strategic perspective, there is the need to understand that local communities are very different, their needs are very different and that you can't develop your centre-based services that cover everyone and hope that they're going to meet all the needs. Service delivery is about looking at that locality working. Sure Start was very localised and what we're trying to do is move back from that but still look at those local areas.

Community participation can greatly help to prioritise and organise services such as pre- and post-natal support, family support through home visits, parent meeting groups, and lifelong learning opportunities. Informed local people become the most effective transmitters of knowledge between communities and services.

Case Study Interview extract 8

Emphasis was on integrated education and childcare places, opening a one-stop shop in one location. What is coming through now is the reality that that can't happen and it isn't the best way to deliver services, The last guidance relaxed on integrated care and education: yes, it can be within a centre, but a centre doesn't necessarily have to have that. It is more about the services provided.

Although services are no longer required to be located together in one building, attention should remain focused on children and families and the locations where they feel comfortable to interact with services. Teams must ask themselves: do the surroundings encourage participation and dialogue? How are meetings with supporting services organised? Are assessments carried out in the places where children and parents feel comfortable? Are services presented in the most effective way? How do multidisciplinary teams come together to share information, to avoid duplication and develop complementary programmes? Buildings which allow meeting rooms alongside provision of the child's regular activities offer clear advantages, but as centres increase in size they will become increasingly forbidding to some parents. The national evaluation of the Sure Start local programmes (NESS, 2006) shows wide variations in the success of local programmes, suggesting that the less disadvantaged communities may have responded more significantly to the programmes offered and consequently been the ones observed to have benefitted most. This finding supports the argument that services need to be finely tuned to meet local needs if they are to prove optimally effective, and this may be best achieved through local participation in governance.

Change from raising educational standards by classroom reform to family support

The early years and childcare strategy was not clearly connected to the national primary strategy until 2003. National and regional foundation stage advisors, whose role was to raise the profile of the foundation stage and support transition and integration between the Foundation Stage and Key Stage 1, were introduced, and curriculum issues began to be integrated more effectively. In 2007 the previously distinct Birth to Three Framework and Foundation Stage were integrated into a unified 0-5 phase linked more clearly to Key Stage 1.

These reforms can be linked to emerging evidence that multi-agency working which targets parents with support and training can have a noticeable impact on school performance. A great deal of this shift in attitude has been facilitated by The Effective Provision of Pre-School Education (EPPE) longitudinal study (Sylva *et al*, 2004). EPPE was commissioned before the Labour government came to power, but fitted very well within the standards agenda. EPPE sought to find out what type of pre-school, if any, might contribute to the achievement of improved outcomes at Key Stage 1. From the early stages of the project certain types of provision were shown to lead to improved transition from nursery into reception (age 4) and subsequently to higher standardised assessment scores at the end of Key Stage 1 (age 7).

The EPPE project emphasised that:

- Integrated centres (centres that fully combine education with care and nursery schools [not classes]) tended to promote better intellectual outcomes for children
- Integrated centres and nursery classes tended to promote better social development even after taking background and prior social behaviour into account
- Disadvantaged children did better in socially mixed centres

Clearly these unfolding findings from the EPPE project have been influential in strengthening the commitment to establishing 3500 children's centres over the next ten years. Policy has moved away from separated education and care settings with supporting services, to integrated service delivery centres. In 2004, however, there was a U-turn in national policy, with the acceptance that children's centres need not be based on a single site. This, I suggest, reflects the financial implications associated with developing new integrated provision and the difficulties of joining up budgets across departments.

This changing view of the importance of early years to educational attainment is picked up in case study extract 9.

Case Study Interview extract 9

It is about putting structures in place so that schools can still continue towards raising standards. I think to be fair, heads recognise this, but it is the time factor. Heads recognise that by having this additional support going in the early years it will support standards by looking at the whole child rather than a bit of the child. That has to be a central policy, but also a local policy to say that is really what we believe in. I do welcome the drive towards quality: we have been very much about a drive towards quantity over the last five years.

Other EPPE findings underscore the need to co-ordinate a range of services to support families in order to improve educational outcomes, and are clearly visible in the development of the Children's Centre Policy and the Workforce Strategy which stresses:

- the importance of the quality of the home learning environment
- the commitment of settings to supporting parents
- well qualified graduate staff
- equal importance given to education and social development
- effective pedagogy seen as involving an equal balance of child-led activity and adult-guided learning.

This emerging evidence should lead to a climate where schools become much more willing partners in developing extended services because they see these services as coinciding with their core aims and targets. Such attitudinal change will in some cases greatly increase the likelihood of initiatives being successful because of improved accommodation and increased co-operation.

Change from increasing access to improving the quality of service provision

Peter Moss praised the first Labour term of office for the 'unparalleled attention and resources devoted to early childhood services' (Moss, 2001, p73). However Moss identified three related policy issues that had not yet been addressed by the childcare strategy:

- Defining what is meant by early childhood (i.e. 0-6 or 3-5)
- Revising the workforce, taking into consideration training, recruitment and retention
- Co-ordinating sustainable funding for early childhood services

Writing with Gunilla Dahlberg at the beginning of the third Labour term of office (Dahlberg and Moss, 2005), Moss identified similar concerns relating to the quality, clarity, direction and focus of early childhood services. This suggests that the Government has avoided difficult financial and political choices related to the integration and quality of education and care provision by devolving them to the local level.

The 2004 Children Act identified recognition that strategies were needed to address these issues, including the revision and integration of the curricular guidance for early years and a workforce strategy that acknowledged pay issues as being closely linked to qualifications and quality. This point has consistently been avoided by national government, leaving a mixed workforce based on affordability ahead of quality. The development of an Early Years Professional Status (EYPS) Qualification developing professionals trained to work in a multi-agency environment is an exciting prospect, but the significant cost implications involved may result in compromises.

The need for agreed working and pay structures in multi-agency teams is clear in Extract 10.

Case Study Interview extract 10

Bring two staffing groups together (childcare and LEA Nursery Staff) when you have them on completely different terms and conditions, with some who work term time only but get higher pay. Because of the way we designed the children's centre building with both a day-care and an LEA nursery provider having instrumental roles in developing open plan design, it then presents difficulties with different staffing teams working together, deploying staff. Bringing a local authority provision with a steady budget coming through, [together with a] provider being a business, understanding that business element of it, and the fact is: that business has got to make money.

We have built on existing provision, which means bringing different management structures together, different staffing structures on different terms and conditions, those sorts of things that we need to work through.

Businesses can only pay a certain amount of money, but then you've got to make a profit, and does there have to be a subsidy to meet the cost of high quality staff? We can't assume people will be happy working together when they have different terms and conditions. Legislation doesn't support us in amalgamating staff because funding streams don't tie up. If the government wants joined-up services in every community they have to legislate to make that happen.

Workforce reforms suggested that training would help staff to share a common workplace language and understanding. Staff moving to better pay and conditions may be more motivated to develop new working practices than staff moving to what they perceive as less favourable working conditions. The radical nature of change should not be underestimated and the culture of the communities of practice that result will be different (see Worsley, chapter 8).

The revision of Ofsted inspections to include the five outcomes identified in the Children Act moves services towards more effective integration of the previously distinct inspection frameworks of childcare and education. The five outcomes recognise holistically that the child has rights to care, mental health and leisure opportunities as well as education, and the outcomes should compel providers to take the agenda of multi-agency working further. The inclusion of rights, enjoyment, entitlements and health and economic outcomes could be used to emphasise the expansion of multi-agency working. These elements have always been present in the childcare strategy but the Children Act once again offers government agencies an opportunity to push this agenda forward where in the past some professionals might have resisted on grounds that it was not within their remit.

Case Study Interview extract 11

I agree that the five outcomes should lead to greater confidence in multi-disciplinary working because the children's centre would be better received in integrated inspection. Station Street would be perceived much more positively than the separated services because it offers support for parents and lifelong learning in addition to the integrated care and education. We are very aware of this as our annual performance assessments are based on how well settings are doing. Time is an issue here as it takes time for all these changes to settle in. There have been so many changes.

So what do these policy changes indicate? Changes in national policy have arisen from the nation's experience of trying to implement the childcare strategy. Change is not simply a matter of government ideology, but rather a manifestation of the interaction between different structural elements of the nation. Each of these changes indicates something of the government's perception about what is important for the nation and what the nation will accept. Local teams and communities must operate within the national framework, but will need to reinterpret these changes to meet their own needs and values.

The change from partnership working in creating childcare places to multi-agency reform in protecting children
The national development of multi-agency working suggests that the ideology of partnership working has not disappeared but that it has given ground to directive working. Government policy on the degree to which it will fund

staffing structures and the training standards it will impose on private and state-funded provision will have a profound effect on the quality of educare offered to children and on the levels of support offered to families.

I have tried to show that in local communities of practice it will be important to try to retain some of the positive elements of voluntary partnership working, such as developing shared aims and values.

Early years knowledge, qualifications and skills have developed over more than half a century to delineate and substantiate the authority of professionals over particular areas of work in order to justify salaries, control and management hierarchies. Changes to these structures will be problematic. Multi-agency advocates have to convince these professional groups that change is going to be effective for children and families. People whose working practices are threatened will need more persuasion.

The change from increasing economic participation in disadvantaged areas to supporting families universally

Government ideology has moved subtly from a belief that individuals needed childcare opportunities to return to work and training in order to improve their cultural, social and economic capital, towards increased concerns about the fragmentation of society and the need to support all families in fostering their children's development. Increased parental leave entitlements show that greater importance is attached to a stable, secure home environment, with the notion that this will in the long term lead to cultural, social and economic improvements. Although the Conservative Party has also pledged themselves to eradicating child poverty by 2020, pessimistic economic forecasts (see Hirsch, 2006) suggest that the number of families living in poverty is unlikely to decrease further through employment opportunities, so that parents being paid for effective parenting might be the most effective strategy for tackling child poverty.

The change from local community involvement to greater national and local government control

This is the most worrying aspect of ideological shift: a strong belief in local community participation has given way to greater imposition of services. The case study illustrates an approach that recognises the value of partnership, local consultation and ownership. Requirements for local governance and accountability set by the government will affect the level of consultation and sense of ownership of services in local communities. Ownership and understanding are important elements of valuing, using and supporting services;

for services to be effective, there has to be trust and understanding. Multi-agency teams owe it to themselves and the communities they serve to make time to spend with others: this may go against their ethical instincts, but the benefits that accrue through improved communication can be significant (see Whitmarsh, chapter 5).

The change from raising educational standards by classroom reform to family support

The multi-agency agenda retains the ideology of raising standards to improve national economic competitiveness. It increasingly offers early intervention as a mechanism for raising standards. This alternative approach to the standards agenda is linked to evidence on the effects of poverty (Feinstein, 2004) and evidence of the effectiveness of early interventions (Sylva *et al*, 2004). Attention is increasingly focused on the whole child, not just their classroom competences, and is manifest in the five outcomes (see Stanley, chapter 7). Multi-agency teams that look at the wider picture in terms of indicators of success such as basic literacy rates, admissions to hospital, or reading levels, are likely to be more viewed as more successful than those which do not. The extent to which the government continues to set targets, and what targets are set, will profoundly affect the ability of teams to perceive the importance of each other's work. Multi-agency teams around the child will do well to keep in mind the broad agenda: the more that individuals can see the bigger picture, the better they will be able to help each other deliver that integrated package of value added service. Effort invested in publishing and sharing local data and experiences within teams may help them see the bigger picture. And seeing the bigger picture may help teams to work to help each other, remembering to signpost each other's services and be more accommodating in times of tension.

The change from increasing access to improving the quality of service provision

The changes in multi-agency working are apparently justified by pragmatic evidence-based approaches to quality; it is nevertheless useful to reflect for a moment on the less apparent ideological underpinnings of change. The changes identified here underscore the Government's belief in the need to compete in a global market place, where skills and technology are seen as the route to preserving jobs and relatively high standards of living. The policy changes discussed offer the promise of better services, but they also offer the possibility of cost savings with revised staffing structures, and rationalisation of service delivery. How the Government chooses to train and fund the staffing structures in multi-agency teams, and the hierarchies and pay structures that result, will have a profound effect on the quality of the services that develop from this reform. The structures developed will indicate where the nation's priorities lie in relation to children's welfare, economic considerations and community reform. These structures will also influence the attitudes of the various stakeholders in multi-agency working towards each other, because of the various power and social relationships that are engendered by the reforms. The desire to leave a lasting legacy and pressures of time may weaken notions of partnership and local participation. The change towards central control at national and local authority level illustrated are important for those implementing multi-agency working to recognise, so that local approaches can be developed that sustain respect and trust between stakeholders into the future. Improved quality will not of itself benefit communities: quality needs also to be accessible and matched to local needs.

Reflective Task

The process of reflection and discourse analysis undertaken in developing this chapter is described more fully by MacNaughton (2005):

> Being reflective means looking back on current practices and seeing how they fit in with how I thought about it years ago and how things are now and how I can change given what is happening now... Inserting critical into critical reflection directs attention away from the individual and towards the operation and effects of power relationships between people. (p6-7)

- Consider how and why changes in your working, learning or home environment have come about.

- What do they indicate about who is in control and what they are seeking to achieve?

- How do they affect your personal situation, to what extent do you share these objectives and how might you wish them to be amended?

References

Anning, A. (2005) Investigating the impact of working in multi-agency service delivery settings in the UK on early years practitioners' beliefs and practices. *Journal of Early Childhood Research* 3(1): 19-50

Bagely, C., Akerly, C., and Rattray, J. (2004) Social Exclusion, Sure Start and organisational capital: evaluating inter-disciplinary multi-agency working in an education and health programme. *Journal of Educational Policy* 19(5): 595-607

Ball, C. (1992) *Start Right.* London, Royal Society of Arts

Barnes, J., Leach, P., Sylva, K., Stein K., Malmberg, L. and the FCCC team (2006) Infant Childcare: Mother's aspirations, actual experiences and the predictors of their satisfaction and confidence in communication with caregivers. *Early Child Development and Care.*176(5)p 553-573

Bronfenbrenner, H. (1979) *The ecology of human development.* Cambridge, Massachusetts: Harvard University Press

CWDC (2006) *Early years professional national Standards*, Children's Workforce Development Unit

Dahlberg, G. and Moss, P. (2005) *Ethics and politics in early childhood education.* London: RoutledgeFalmer

Department for Education and Science (DfES) (2006) *The common assessment framework for children and young people; practitioners' guide.* London: Department for Education and Skills

Department for Education and Science (DfES) (2004) *Choice for parents; the best start for children. A ten year strategy for childcare* Nottingham, Department for Education and Skills

Esland, G. (1996) Knowledge and Nationhood: the New Right, Education and the Global Market. In Avis J., Bloomer, M., Esland, G., Gleeson, D., Hodkinson, P (1996) *Knowledge and Nationhood.* London: Cassell

Feinstein, L., Duckworth, K., and Sabates, R. (2004) *A model of Intergenerational transmission of educational success.* London, The Centre for Research on the Wider Benefits of Learning: Institute of Education

Glass, N. (2005) Surely Some Mistake *Guardian Society* 5 January 2005

Hirsch, D. (2006) *What will it take to end child poverty?*York, Joseph Rowntree Trust

Laming (2003) *The Victoria Climbié Inquiry Summary and Recommendations.* Norwich, HMSO

Leach, P., Barnes, J., Nichols, M., Goldin, J., Stein, A., Sylva, K., Malmberg, L. (2006) Child care before 6 months of age. *Infant and Child Development* Vol.15 No.5 pp471-502

National Evaluation of Sure Start (NESS) (2006) *Changes in the Characteristics of SSLP area between 2001/2 and 2003/4.* Nottingham: Department for Education and Skills

MacNaughton, G. (2005) *Doing Foucault in Early Childhood Studies.* Abingdon: Routledge

Moss, P. (2001) Renewed hopes and lost opportunities: Early childhood in the early years of the Labour government. in M. Fielding (2001) *Taking education really seriously: Four years hard Labour.* London: RoutledgeFalmer

Schweinhart, L. J. (1993) Summary of the Effects of the Perry Group Program thru age 27. in C. Ball. (1993) *Start Right.* London: Royal Society of Arts

Sylva, K., Melhuish, E., Sammons, P., Siraj-Blatchford, I. and Taggart, B. (2004) *The final report: effective pre-school education.* London, Institute of Education University of London

Tunstill, J., Allnock, D., Akehurst, S., and Garbers, C. (2005) 'Sure Start local programmes: Implications of case study data from the national evaluation of sure start.' *Children and Society* 19: 158-171

Weinberger, J., Pickstone, C. and Hannon, P. (2005) *Learning from Sure Start.* Maidenhead: Open University Press

5

Negotiating the moral maze: developing ethical literacy in multi-agency settings

Judith Whitmarsh

Introduction

This chapter takes the somewhat abstract notion of ethics and explores its relevance to contemporary practice in the early years, specifically in relation to multi-agency working. It aims to show that ethics is not a dense, philosophical, theoretical concept nor the slavish adherence to a professional code, but that an understanding of basic ethics can clarify problems and help us make decisions that will enhance our practice and our research. The chapter shows how an understanding of ethics can illuminate issues and dilemmas that arise for practitioners, parents and children, and offer some signposts towards joint ethical working. To sum up, ethics concerns the basic values that underpin our relationships with others, whether in a professional or personal context; developing 'ethical literacy' enables us to identify where we, as a multi-agency team, are coming from and to clarify how we can move forward.

Where tensions exist in multi-agency working, they are often caused by misunderstandings about shared language, shared information and mutual practices relating to them. Therefore, first we need to clarify what we mean by ethics and ethical practice: the first section offers a brief history of ethics, exploring the sources of our modern interpretations and how the past influences the present. Next, the why of ethics and ethical practice are investigated: why are ethics important? Why can we not just follow our professional codes and consider our practice therefore to be ethical? The chapter then explores the ethical concept of confidentiality from the perspective of three different disciplines: education, nursing and social work. It shows how professionals from different disciplines may interpret confidentiality differently. Finally, we need to make some decisions about how to develop a joint model of ethical practice that caters for professionals from a variety of backgrounds, for parents, families and, of course, the children who are at the heart of our work. This chapter draws on examples from real-life practice. All names and identifying features have been changed.

Ethical codes of practice

Ethical discussion began with the Ancient Greek philosophers Aristotle, Plato and Socrates. All had meaningful and useful things to say that have informed contemporary ethics. Socrates, for example, devoted his life to a search for the truth about the right way to live (Hogan, 2005, p185). Hogan further argues that Platonic searches for the truth became the foundation for much institutionalised educational thinking, thus the truth became a prescriptive doctrine that headed Christian education through the centuries (Hogan, 2005). Scott (1995) suggests that Aristotle's virtue theory can be applied to healthcare ethics. She maintains that from Aristotelian theory we learn that any discussion should begin from what is known about the issues (reflection), followed by clarification of the ethical problem and, finally, consideration of possible ways of addressing the issues. This three-point model would be a useful framework for any potential discussion of an ethical dilemma:

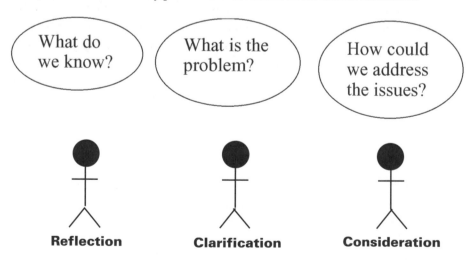

What do we know?	What is the problem?	How could we address the issues?
Reflection	**Clarification**	**Consideration**

Moving on to more recent times, eighteenth century philosophers such as Kant and Hume critiqued notions of truth, arguing against the metaphysical ideal, which holds that there is one scientific truth that can be observed, held and accounted for. Thus in contemporary modern thought, stances such as postmodernism promote the concept of the truth as relative, conditional and contextual.

Sara is manager of the Children's Centre. She employs Janet as a nursery nurse. There is an incident, observed by a parent, who states that Janet had been snappy all morning, curt to the children and grabbed Rehaan from the climbing frame, leaving red marks on his arms. Sara needs to find out the truth. Janet denies being snappy and curt; she argues that the parent 'has it in for her' and says that she grabbed Rehaan because she spotted a wasp on the climbing frame just where he was about to place his hand. Whose truth should Sara believe?

Incidents like this demonstrate how the truth can vary, depending on perspective. But if the truth can vary so much, how are we to offer guidance for ethical practice? This relativism is addressed later.

Medical ethics date from Hippocrates, although modern ethics are seen to originate in the nineteenth century (Homan, 1991). The uncovering of Nazi war crimes that masqueraded as medical research led to the development of The Nuremberg Code. This makes it clear that voluntary informed consent is an essential part of good practice in research of any nature (Farrell, 2005). The Nuremberg Code appeared to safeguard public interests until the 1970s, when attention was drawn to several medical and psychological research studies that were exposed as unethical (Gross, 1991). Psychological research by Milgram (1974), Zimbardo *et al* (1973) and Hofling *et al* (1966) all raised questions about what was meant by ethical research and research conduct. The ethical problems raised during this era led the US government to establish the National Commission for the Protection of Human Subjects in Biomedical and Behavioral Research, who, in turn, produced the *Belmont Report* (1979). From their study of the many codes of conduct and of ethics, the Belmont Report noted three common, basic principles: respect for persons, beneficence – doing good and minimising harm – and justice. These principles were considered equal in importance and were subsequently adopted by the Council for International Organisations of Medical Sciences and its later affiliate, the World Health Organisation (Ensign, 2003). Thus modern-day ethics have their roots in bio-medical scientific research. It is noteworthy that informed consent, confidentiality, privacy and anonymity are seen as integral to the principles of respect, beneficence and justice, whereas much contemporary understanding of ethics focuses on these as separate issues.

What do we mean by ethics?

Ethics is a contested term: most definitions relate, in some sense or other, to guidance about what is considered to be a right and proper way to behave. Gregory (2003, p2) argues that the terms 'ethics' and 'morals' can and should be used interchangeably, whereas Homan (1991, p1) is more specific and argues that 'ethics is the science of morality: those who engage in it determine values for the regulation of human behaviour'. Dahlberg and Moss (2005, p66) have perhaps the most practical and useful definition for early years professionals, when they state that ethics is the 'should question: how should we think and act?'

This raises questions about who decides the right way to think and act. If professionals believe they are acting in an ethical manner, does that make their practice ethical? In order to explore these complex issues further, we need to evaluate the underpinning principles and theories, argued over for centuries by some of the greatest philosophers.

Principles of ethics

The three principles that underpin most codes of ethics are:

- Respect for persons: protecting the autonomy of persons, with courtesy and respect for individuals
- Beneficence: maximising good outcomes for science, humanity and the individual while avoiding or minimising unnecessary harm, risk or wrong
- Justice: reasonable, non-exploitative, fair behaviour (adapted from Farrell, 2005, p4)

However, no code of ethics can lay down detailed, absolute guidance for all the complexities that arise during professional practice and research. In some instances, competing moral claims leave the practitioner with an ethical dilemma about which principle is more important than the other (see box opposite).

There are a number of ethical issues here: first, does the mother have the right to contravene first-aid policy in the setting? Secondly, does the teacher/first-aider have the right to treat Jamie in contravention of his parent's wishes? Thirdly, what effect would the correctly imposed treatment have on a) Jamie's

Jamie, four years old, had a nose-bleed in nursery school. His teacher followed the first-aid guidelines and encouraged Jamie to put his head slightly forward and pinch the soft tissue of his nostrils. This stopped the nose-bleed. The following day, Jamie's mother sent an angry letter to the head-teacher stating that:

- Her family are prone to nose-bleeds
- She has taught Jamie to pinch the bridge of his nose
- She wants him to deal with his nose-bleeds as she has taught him
- She refuses permission for staff to treat him otherwise

wellbeing and b) Jamie's relationship with his mother? Referring back to the ethical principles we need to consider:

- respect for both Jamie and his mother
- the mother's right to autonomy and to make decisions about the welfare of her child
- the head teacher's responsibility to avoid or minimise risk and harm to a child
- the headteacher's respect for the first-aid knowledge of the teacher and need to protect the teacher from risk and harm
- Jamie's right to autonomy and to make decisions about treatment that involves his body. Would the teacher be justified in treating Jamie if he refused it?

In this particular case, the competing claims appeared difficult to resolve. Eventually, after negotiation, the mother agreed that Jamie could pinch his nose, as she wished, in the first instance but if the nose-bleed continued for more than a couple of minutes, the teacher would then take over the first-aid. The mother signed a form to this effect. The school is currently considering running first-aid classes for parents and introducing it into the curriculum for pupils.

This particular case introduces the notion that ethical principles may be different to rules and policies: rules tend to be specific (for example, the first-aid treatment for nosebleeds is...) and less open to interpretation, but the ethical principles underpin the rules (Pring, 2001). Underlying the nosebleed treatment rules are the principles of 'not doing harm' and 'maximising a good outcome'. Thus principles include values: the nosebleed rules tell us what to do practically, but the ethical principles give us guidance about what is moral and ethical to do in this situation.

The trouble with codes of ethics

Codes serve a useful purpose as a guide to the ethical behaviour desired by professional bodies, in fact the code of ethics is often seen as 'one of the defining features of a profession' (Banks, 2001, p84). Some professional codes have more power than others: transgressions can lead to the ultimate sanction of removal from the profession. However, as we observed in Jamie's case, codes do not necessarily give us all the answers and, as multi-disciplinary teams become more common in the early years, some codes may conflict with others in their interpretation, as the examples below demonstrate:

■ Hardeep is a recently qualified health visitor attached to the Children's Centre. She abides by the Nursing and Midwifery Council Code of Practice (NMC, 2002) and is never quite sure how much confidential information about family health issues she should share with the other team members. She is always very cautious; she tends to get her clinical manager's approval to release health information and this delays action and the rest of the team find this delay difficult

■ Tony is a social worker; although careful about client information, his code suggests that this can be shared on a 'need to know' basis and he sees Hardeep's attitude as obstructive, even dangerous, if he has suspicions of child protection issues. He is becoming frustrated with the problem

■ Marge is a nursery nurse with 20 years' experience. While she is careful about record-keeping, she is always ready to share her knowledge of the crèche parents and children at the team meetings, if required. She follows ethical principles of respect and is careful of client privacy

---

Rodd (2005) notes the limited impact of ethical codes on the advocacy of children's rights. And while she claims that an ethical code can 'provide guiding principles for decision-making' (p141), she acknowledges that ethical codes do not 'attempt to provide prescriptive or 'right' answers to the complex questions and ethical dilemmas faced by early childhood practitioners' (p142). Furthermore, educational philosophers (see, for example, Greenbank, 2004; Hodkinson, 2004; Homan, 1991) argue that strict adherence to codes can discourage exploration of the values and morality of practice and inhibit morally responsible behaviour.

French (see chapter 3) demonstrates how issues of information-sharing and confidentiality frequently create barriers to multi-agency working. Could this be because confidentiality, although not a *prima facie* principle of ethics, is laid down in professional codes and may be thought to have legal ramifications (these are discussed in the final section of this chapter)? Breaching confidentiality therefore, whether consciously or inadvertently, carries risks: sharing information then becomes a risky enterprise. Farrell (2005, p2) suggests that the emergence of ethical codes is a response to an increasing concern with risk, requiring 'heightened accountability, regulation and surveillance'. If children are seen to inhabit a 'risky space' (Farrell, 2005, p3), it is little surprise that the practitioners responsible for their care and education feel themselves vulnerable guardians of a risky enterprise, particularly when ascribed codes do not offer solutions to their ethical dilemmas.

Cultural influences

We have noted that the study of ethics should give us guidance about how to relate to others in a moral way; we have also identified the fact that ethical discourse engages with values and with notions of the truth. This assumes that there is a 'right' way to think and act. But are we sure that our own understandings of the 'right' way and 'truth' are universal? How do we manage our interactions when child, family and other practitioners may have a different understanding of the 'right' way?

Becoming more inclusive

Fleer (2006) draws our attention to the way in which the early childhood centre may not reflect the cultural values and practices of home, school and work. She argues that culturally diverse values and practices need to be integrated and addressed within early years practice and not merely 'added on to mainstream fundamental early childhood education' (p.136).

Jenny French (in chapter 3) describes the history and development of the current child-centred pedagogy. She demonstrates how service providers have been required to make a shift to family- and child-centred provision, placing their needs at the heart of professional practice. This may, however, require a shift in the underlying values of multi-agency practitioners. Can we really adapt our own values systems to incorporate diverse, or even opposing, parental beliefs? Clarke and French (see chapter 9) highlight how successful partnerships depend on practitioners' ability to accept changes that may be necessary within themselves. In a multi-agency team, the core ethical beliefs and values of the team may be as diverse as those of the general population.

Tackling this dilemma requires us to stop thinking in dualistic terms: that is to halt the dialectic in which something is either true or it is not. Instead, we need to begin thinking more in terms of ethical behaviour as an interaction which can vary according to its context (as we saw in the vignette of Jamie). Considering ethical practice as relational opens up spaces in which we can discuss the issues while trying to weigh up which principle may, on this occasion, be of over-riding use to the specific situation. If we stop thinking in terms of a polarised duality, an either/or situation, we can begin to search for shared understanding. Most of our deeply held values are on a continuum and we will undoubtedly share some of the underlying constituents with others. We can begin by seeking out the similarities during discussion, rather than the differences.

Jackson (2006) suggests that ethical inquiry could begin with developing a consensus on what is not ethical practice and behaviour: identifying this may lead to agreement about what ethical practice would look like. Sharing experiences of ethical dilemmas can feel threatening, so developing ethical literacy may initially be easier if it is not too personal. Setting a few ground rules at the beginning of the discussion, perhaps about privacy, may help those present to feel safer. One way to de-personalise a dilemma is to reframe it for discussion as an anonymous vignette, much as this chapter has done. The three-point model from this chapter could be used to help structure the discussion.

An alternative might be to present a hypothetical issue for discussion or to explore the team's understandings of such concepts as informed consent, information sharing, or the difference between privacy and confidentiality. As practitioners become more at ease with the exploration of ethics, they may themselves raise personal dilemmas.

Moving into an ethical space may enable practitioners to explore taken-for-granted beliefs and practices in order to build an ethos and practice that can encompass diversity. Within that ethical space, we need to listen to parents, carers, families and practitioners, to create a dialogic relationship as a first step along our ethical pathway.

Reviewing the situation
So far, we have considered the origins of ethics and its recent development. This led us into a consideration of ethical principles and an understanding that ethical codes, while useful, may not be able to resolve all the increasingly complex potential dilemmas arising in multi-agency working. If we cannot find simple, straightforward answers to ethical problems, then we need to develop innovative ways of engaging with the issues in order to enable a

multi-disciplinary workforce to share understandings and to support each other. One way forward is to avoid thinking in dualisms of either 'I am right and they are wrong', or 'there is one right answer to my problem' and begin to move into the concept of spaces for shared ethical discussion, realising that there may be a number of conflicting priorities, competing ethical principles, and a number of possible solutions; in other words, thinking about ethics as an ongoing process. If we consider ethics as relational, as the basis of our relationships with others, as re-conceptualising our understanding of ethics it will prepare us for engaging with a personal process of developing ethical literacy. As Martin Needham suggests (chapter 4), the more individuals can see the bigger picture, the better they will be able to help each other deliver the integrated package. We now move into the final section – an exploration of one of the commonest causes of tension in multi-agency working: sharing information.

Sharing information within an ethical space

As noted earlier, sharing information is one of the commonest causes of tension in multi-agency teams (Dahl and Aubrey, 2004; Rowe, 2003; Newman, 2000) and frequently perspectives between groups of professionals differ (Dahl et al, 2005; Milbourne et al, 2003; Atkinson et al, 2002; Anning, 2001; Jones, 2000). It is of such importance to successful multi-agency working that the government is currently consulting on the issues in order to inform future practice (DfES, 2005a). Every Child Matters: Change for Children (DfES, 2004) and the draft statutory guidelines on the Children Act (2004) set out a duty to co-operate and clear expectations for cross-agency information-sharing (see earlier chapters for an extended discussion). At the heart of information-sharing lies the concept of confidentiality, and the following section explores this from the viewpoint of an educationalist, a nursing practitioner and a social worker.

Confidentiality and the teacher

Within the discipline of education, confidentiality is most commonly invoked in child protection procedures and in research. The courts have found a common law duty of confidence to exist where, 'there is a special relationship between parties, such as patient-doctor, solicitor-client, teacher-pupil' (DfES, 2005a, Appendix 1: 2.1). However, this consultation document states that the duty is not absolute and information may be shared when:

- the information is not confidential in nature
- the person to whom the duty is owed has implicitly or explicitly authorised the disclosure

- there is over-riding public interest in disclosure
- disclosure is ordered by a court order or other legal obligation

In a potential child protection case, the guidelines lay out a clear pathway of procedure and the child's best interests must over-ride the duty of confidentiality (see for example DfES, 2005b). Few teachers would find difficulties in breaching confidentiality to support an abused child; however, there may be occasions when education practitioners suspect that all is not well, but have no clear-cut evidence of abuse. Many teachers observing cuts and bruises on a child are unsure if these have a natural explanation: children fall over and accumulate injuries through their adventurous and exploratory activities, and young children may not be able to give a clear answer about the origins of injuries. Children have off periods when they may appear unhappy or withdrawn, without necessarily being subject to abuse. Child protection is a risky business, both for the child and the caring adult; teachers, afraid of getting it wrong, anticipate trial by tabloid, disciplinary action, and the worst possible outcome: the death of a pupil. It is little surprise that, as McCullough observes (see chapter 2), some practitioners prefer to pass any responsibility for child protection on to nominated local services.

We commented earlier about Farrell's (2005) concerns that the increase in ethical codes may originate from an increased perception of children inhabiting a risky environment; we also note that this risky environment encompasses the adults working within it. How can we minimise the perceived risks?

The advent of the Children Act 2004 and the Every Child Matters policy documentation (described earlier in more detail by my colleagues) supports the development of the lead professional in cases of complex need, the development of multi-agency working and the keystone of information-sharing. Ethics and ethical practice underpin these concepts: by becoming increasingly ethically literate, practitioners can share their understanding of confidentiality and their fears and anxieties in a non-threatening space. By considering vignettes of potential child protection scenarios, searching out ethical principles for consideration, and debating risk, we can develop greater confidence in our practice.

Confidentiality and the nurse

Nursing guidelines on confidentiality are framed within a professional code of practice and those who do not follow the guidelines are liable to disciplinary action. The Code of Professional Conduct for nurses states clearly:

■ 5.1: You must treat information about patients and clients as confidential and use it only for the purpose for which it was given. As it is impractical to obtain consent every time you need to share information with others, you should ensure that patients and clients understand that some information may be made available to members of the team involved in the delivery of care. You must guard against breaches of confidentiality by protecting information from improper disclosure at all times

■ 5.2: If you are required to disclose information outside the team that will have personal consequences for patients or clients, you must obtain their consent. If the patient or client withholds consent, or if consent cannot be obtained for whatever reason, disclosures may only be made where:

■ They can be justified in the public interest (usually where disclosure is essential to protect the patient or client or someone else from the risk of significant harm)

■ They are required by law or by order of a court. (Nursing and Midwifery Council (NMC), 2002, p7)

This appears to give strong, explicit guidance to nurses, midwives and health visitors. However it raises questions about who is a member of a team: do we include the voluntary workers in the setting? Does the team consist of all the NHS workers: health visitors, midwives, speech therapists, child and adult mental health services and psychologists? How much information can be given to teachers, the early years staff, to the educational psychologist, to the police, Citizens Advice Bureau, the housing department who may be on site? In order to clarify these issues, the NMC are currently advising nurses and midwives to participate in the Department for Education and Skills consultation on information sharing in multi-agency settings, although this consultation applies only to England and not to other areas of the United Kingdom. This consultation (DfES, 2005a) proposes that a two-tier system may enable the health professional to indicate a concern about a child, as a first measure, without revealing the identity of the child and the circumstances of the concern. The second tier would allow the sharing of confidential information, without consent if necessary, to safeguard the child's interest, for example in a child protection case.

Confidentiality and the social worker
Let us now consider how a social worker might respond to information sharing and confidentiality.

Clark (2000) describes both a strong and a weak version of confidentiality. In the strong version, nothing the client communicates to the social worker should be passed on to others unless 'good reasons are shown to the contrary' (p186). Clark's weak version proposes that client information can be passed on to others but in a way that does not reveal the identity of the client. Thus a case-history, with all identifying features removed, could be passed to a team member for comment and advice. However Clark then describes how much identifiable client information is

> ...inspected by managers and consulted by supervisors and colleagues who may have to deal with the case in the worker's absence. In practice, files are usually available on demand to virtually any professional member of the agency, even if they have no clear cause for viewing a file. (p187)

Open-plan offices, minimal privacy, and informal conversation and gossip all militate against true confidentiality in social work client affairs (Clark, 2000).

Banks (2001) notes how the title 'social worker' covers a diverse range of settings so defining conceptual rules for confidentiality may have different applications in different circumstances. The social worker may belong to a statutory agency or a voluntary agency; they may be attached to a children's centre, a residential unit, an adoption agency or even a rape crisis centre, to name a few. The level of confidentiality may have different importance when dealing with different clients such as people with HIV, offenders, child protection, adoption, or in an independent counselling agency. Banks (2001, p109) argues that

> The most appropriate statement that might be made about confidentiality ... might be that social workers should ensure that their agencies have policies and codes of practice clearly stating the extent to which information given by the user to a social worker will and will not be kept confidential.

Resolving information-sharing dilemmas

The law about confidentiality and sharing information rests on three legal frameworks: the Common Law Duty of Confidence, the Human Rights Act 1998, and the Data Protection Act 1998. The increasingly complex issues regarding confidentiality, viewed – incorrectly – by many as an absolute right in the doctor-patient relationship, have led to the British Medical Association statement that 'patient confidentiality is desirable but not an absolute concept and can be breached if circumstances warrant such action' (BMA, 2004, p3). Montgomery (2003, p270) suggests that 'it is difficult to show that a legal obligation exists' in relation to sharing information about child protection issues, yet it has become part of professional good practice.

This brings us back to the problems of assuming that a policy or code of ethics will answer all our questions about the right way to behave. As this chapter has demonstrated, complex ethical dilemmas require more than a one size fits all ethical code, particularly in multi-agency practice. Banks (2001) proposes that social workers need to develop a capacity to become reflective about their work and its ethical dimensions, which returns us to our notion of ethical spaces:

> Do we want professionals to become more than simply rule-following automata? We do want to develop people who respect confidentiality because they are the kind of people who are trustworthy and respectful in all aspects of life, not just because their agency or professional association has laid down a rule to this effect. (Banks, 2001, p54)

A multi-disciplinary discussion of professional understandings of confidentiality could draw on guidance from cross-government guidance (DfES, 2005a) to develop shared reference points on which to build a common understanding of information-sharing and confidentiality. As Nunney notes, 'No inquiry into a child's death or serious injury has ever questioned why information was shared. It has always asked the opposite' (DfES, 2006, p3).

The Department for Education and Skills (2006, p4) suggests that the following principles underpin decisions to share information:

- Is there a legitimate purpose for you or your agency to share the information?
- Does the information enable a person to be identified?
- Is the information confidential?
- Is so, do you have consent to share?
- Is there a statutory duty or court order to share the information?
- If consent is refused, or there are good reasons not to seek consent, is there a sufficient public interest to share information?
- If the decision is to share, are you sharing the information in the right way?
- Have you properly recorded your decision?

(For further details, see www.ecm.gov.uk/informationsharing)

This brief discussion demonstrates how our understanding of just one key ethical concept, confidentiality, raises a number of questions that will need addressing in a multi-agency setting. The discussion has not begun to engage with issues of autonomy, informed consent, privacy, accountability and anonymity, although these are all inherent within the vignettes: for Jamie's carers, accountability is an over-riding ethical principle; for Hardeep, Tony and Marge, information-sharing is of key importance, for others, child protection may be the over-riding concern. Each profession will have its own knowledge base, its own code-related guidelines, and its own understanding of these. By sharing knowledge, we can perhaps further our understanding of each other's ethical background in order to become ethically literate.

Conclusion

While this chapter has not provided quick-fix answers, it offers some ways to approach ethical dilemmas. Ethical codes offer guidance in professional situations, but they can also inhibit ethical behaviour by their inflexibility. Furthermore, the wide variety of professionals involved in multi-agency working may each have their own code emphasising different rules, principles and values. The voluntary workers and non-professional staff may be left floundering, unsure whose ethical code is paramount.

Moving away from a dualist, polarised way of thinking about ethics, in which there is a right and a wrong answer, and suggesting that ethical codes may be useful in simple situations but cannot respond to complexity, leaves us with our own ethical dilemma: how then do we resolve a situation that appears to have inherent conflicting and competing demands? Our assumptions about what is right and wrong can be culturally determined and historically mediated: can we be sure that children, families and other professionals share our personal viewpoint and, if not, how do we encompass diverse values and beliefs?

The answer to this must lie in the development of reflective, non-critical spaces (Dahlberg and Moss, 2005) in which we explore the labyrinth of ethics and ethical principles and develop our own frameworks for ethical behaviour. Jackson (2006, p4) observes that 'the central question in ethics is: how ought we to live our lives?' New ways of multi-agency working require new ways of thinking and the development of new professional relationships; developing ethical literacy will enable us to make sound, shared decisions about how we want to live our professional lives.

Reflective Task

Review some of the case studies with other people and share your opinions about how to respond to them.

References

Anning, A. (2001) 'Knowing who I am and what I know: developing new versions of professional knowledge in integrated service settings'. In British Educational Research Association conference. University of Leeds, UK. 13-15 September 2001. http://www.leeds.ac.uk/educol/documents/00001877.htm

Atkinson, M. Wilkin, A. Stott, A. Doherty, P. and Kinder, K. (2002) Multi-agency working: a detailed study. Slough, NFER

Banks, S. (2001) *Ethics and Values in Social Work. 2nd ed.* Basingstoke: Palgrave

The Belmont Report (1978) Ethical Principles and Guidelines for the Protection of Human Subjects of Research. Washington: Department of Health, Education and Welfare. In Small, R. (2001) Codes are Not Enough: What Philosophy can Contribute to the Ethics of Educational Research. *Journal of Philosophy of Education*, 35(3), pp. 387-406

British Medical Association (2004) 'Confidentiality and disclosure of health information'. http//:www.bma.org.uk

Clark, CL. (2000) *Social Work Ethic: Politics, Principles and Practice.* Basingstoke: Palgrave

Clarke, J. Gewirtz, S. and McLaughlin, E. (eds.) (2000) *New Managerialism, New Welfare?* London: Sage Publications with Open University Press

Coady, M. Ethics in early childhood research. In Mac Naughton, G. Rolfe, SA. and Siraj-Blatchford, I. (eds.) (2001) *Doing Early Childhood Research: International Perspectives on Theory and Practice.* Buckingham: Open University Press, pp64-75

Dahl, S. and Aubrey, C. (2004) Multi-agency working in Sure Start projects: Successes and Challenges. In British Educational Research Association Early Years Special Interest Group. University of Warwick, UK, May 27 2004

Dahl, S., Clarke, L. and Aubrey, C. (2005) Factors facilitating and Hindering Partnership working: Findings from Sure Start Local Programmes in Coventry. Draft report. In Sharing Research in Early Childhood: 'A Multi-professional Approach to Education and Childcare: Critical Reflections. University of Warwick, UK, 2005, March 20-23, 2005

Dahlberg, G. and Moss, P. (2005) *Ethics and Politics in Early Childhood Education.* Abingdon: RoutledgeFalmer

Department for Education and Science (DfES) (2006) *Making It Happen: Working together for children and young people.* Mailbox.isadivision@DfES.gsi.gov.uk

Department for Education and Science (DfES) (2005a) *Cross-government guidance: sharing information on children and young people.* Runcorn: DfES

Department for Education and Science (DfES) (2005b) *What to do if you're worried a child is being abused: summary.* London: Department for Education and Skills

Department for Education and Science (DfES) (2004) *Every Child Matters: Change for Children.* Nottingham: DfES

Department for Education and Science (DfES) (2004) *Children Act.* London: The Stationery Office.

Ensign, J. (2003) Ethical issues in qualitative health research with homeless youths. *Journal of Advanced Nursing*, 43(1), pp43-50

Farrell, A. (2005) (Ed) *Ethical Research with Children.* Buckingham: Open University Press

Fleer, M. (2006) The cultural construction of child development: creating institutional and cultural intersubjectivity. *International Journal of Early years Education*, 14(2), June, pp127-140

Greenbank, P. (2004) The Role of Values in Educational Research: the case for reflexivity. *British Educational Research Journal*, 29(6), pp791-801

Gregory, I. (2003) *Ethics in Research*. London: Continuum.

Gross, R. (1991) *Psychology: The Science of Mind and Behaviour*. London: Hodder and Stoughton

Hodkinson, P. (2004) Research as a form of work: expertise, community and methodological objectivity. *British Education Research Journal*, 30(1), February 2004, pp9-26

Hofling, KC. Brotzman, E. Dalrymple, S. Graves, N. and Pierce, CM. (1966) An experimental study in the nurse-physician relationship. *Journal of Mental Disorders*,143, pp. 171-180. Cited in Gross, R. (1991) *Psychology: The Science of Mind and Behaviour*. London: Hodder and Stoughton

Hogan, P. (2005) The integrity of learning and the search for truth. *Educational Theory*. 55(2), pp185-200

Homan, R. (1991) *The Ethics of Social Research*. Harlow: Longman

Homan, R. (2001) The Principle of Assumed Consent. *Journal of Philosophy of Education*, 35(3), August 2001, pp329-344

Jackson, J. (2006) *Ethics in Medicine*. Cambridge: Polity Press

Jones, H. (2000) 'Partnerships: a common sense approach to inclusion?' In SCUTREA, 30th Annual Conference. University of Nottingham, UK. 3-5 July 2000. http://www.leeds.ac.uk/educol/documents/00001456.htm

Milbourne, L. Macrae, S. and Maguire, M. (2003) Collaborative solutions or new policy problems: exploring multi-agency partnerships in education and health work. *Journal of Education Policy*, 18(1), pp19-35

Milgram, S. (1974) Obedience to authority. New York: Harper and Row. Cited in Gross, R. (1991) *Psychology: The Science of Mind and Behaviour*. London: Hodder and Stoughton

Montgomery, J. (2003) *Health Care Law. (2nd edition)* Oxford: Oxford University Press

Newman, J (2000) Beyond the New Public Management? Modernizing Public Services. In Clarke, J. Gewirtz, S. and McLaughlin, E. (eds.) (2000) *New Managerialism, New Welfare?* London: Sage Publications with Open University Press, pp45-61

Nunney, G. (2006) Quotation cited in DfES (2006) *Making It Happen: Working together for children and young people*. Mailbox.isadivision@DfES.gsi.gov.uk p3

Nursing and Midwifery Council (2006) The NMC code under review. *NMC Quarterly Publication*, 14, January, p5

Nursing and Midwifery Council (2002) Code of professional conduct: standards for conduct, performance and ethics. (Online). London: Nursing and Midwifery Council. http://www.nmc-uk.org

Pring, R. (2001) The Virtues and Vices of an Educational Researcher. *Journal of Philosophy of Education*, 35(3), pp407-421

Rodd, J. (2005) *Leadership in Early Childhood. (3rd ed)* Buckingham: Open University Press

Rowe, A. (2003) *An evaluation of the involvement of health visitors in the Sure Start Foxhill and Parson Cross programme*. (Online). Sheffield University. (Accessed 7.1.05). http://www.sheffield.ac.uk/surestart/publns.html

Scott, PA. (1995) Aristotle, Nursing and Health Care Ethics. *Nursing Ethics*. 2(4), pp279-285

UK Parliament (1998) *The Data Protection Act*. London: The Stationery Office

UK Parliament (1998) *The Human Rights Act*. London: The Stationery Office

Zimbardo, PG. Banks, WC. Craig, H. and Jaffe, D. (1973) A Pirandellian prison: the mind is a formidable jailor. In *New York Times magazine*, April 8, pp. 38-60

6

Leadership in multi-agency work

Bernadette Duffy and Janice Marshall

Introduction

During the last few years we have seen a dramatic increase in the number of centres and schools operating with multi-agency teams. It has been a period of rapid change, and as there are plans to develop more children's centres and extended schools, all the signs are that the pace of change for early years practitioners is likely to increase rather than diminish. These developments have led to changes in the way that leadership is viewed in early years settings. Where once a head teacher or head of centre was seen primarily as a good practitioner who would lead the team through example, the expectation now is that a head will be, in Office for Standards in Education (Ofsted) language, the 'chief inspector of their school/centre', employing a range of strategies to promote the best outcomes for children and distributing leadership among the whole staff team. While many of these changing expectations have been welcome and have enhanced rigour, clarity and direction, they have also presented challenges and raised issues which need to be recognised and addressed.

In this chapter we look at the nature of leadership in multi-agency teams. We draw on our experience of integrated centres over the last 25 years, especially our recent experience at the Thomas Coram Centre for Children and Families in Camden where we currently act as Head of Centre and Deputy Head. We also draw on Janice's experiences while completing the National Professional Qualification of Integrated Centre Leadership (NPQICL).

The areas we focus on are:

- the expectations now placed on leaders
- the challenges and issues in multi-agency team work
- our approach at Thomas Coram
- successful leadership of multi-agency teams

Changing expectations

The last ten years have seen a changing profile for early years services in Britain. The importance of the early years of childhood, and the potential of settings to improve children's lives in the here and now as well as their prospects for the future is recognised (HMT, 2004). Alongside this growing recognition has come increasing evidence that the best way to develop early years services is through multi-agency teams. The range of services now offered by a multi-agency setting can include:

- integrated educating and care for children from babies to five year olds, ten hours per day, 48 weeks per year,
- support for children with a range of additional needs
- family support including drop-ins, home visiting, specialist groups, for example for young parents
- adult education
- health services such as health visiting, speech therapy and psychology
- employment and training opportunities including links with Job Centre Plus
- training and support for practitioners

The Government's national strategy has changed the landscape of early years service and led to the development of Sure Start local programmes, Early Excellence Centres and now children's centres and extended schools. The early years have become an integral part of the Government's strategy for tackling social exclusion. For the Government the main purpose of children's centres is to improve outcomes for young children in line with *Every Child Matters* (DfES, 2004), with a particular focus on the most disadvantaged (DfES, 2005a).

With this responsibility has come greater accountability and the need for effective leadership in early childhood settings, and the Self Evaluation Form (SEF) that schools now complete reflects this. The form has been produced by Ofsted (Ofsted, 2005) and section six, on leadership and management, asks leadership teams to answer the following questions:

What is the overall effectiveness and efficiency of leadership and management?

- how effectively leaders and managers at all levels set clear direction leading to improvement, and promote high quality of integrated care and education

- how effectively performance is monitored and improved to meet challenging targets through quality assurance and self-assessment

- how well equality of opportunity is promoted and discrimination tackled so that all learners achieve their potential (i.e. inclusion)

- the adequacy and suitability of staff, specialist equipment, learning resources and accommodation

- how effectively and efficiently resources are deployed to achieve value for money

- how effectively links are made with other providers, services, employers and other organisations to promote the integration of care, education and any extended services to enhance learning

- the extent to which governors (and, if appropriate, other supervisory boards) discharge their responsibilities

- the adequacy and suitability of staff, specialist equipment, learning resources and accommodation

- how effectively and efficiently resources are deployed to achieve value for money

- how effectively links are made with other providers, services, employers and other organisations to promote the integration of care, education and any extended services to enhance learning

- the extent to which governors (and, if appropriate, other supervisory boards) discharge their responsibilities

(Ofsted, 2005)

This is a very different set of questions to those Bernadette was asked when she first applied for headship back in the 1980s. Then the questions asked at interview focused on the curriculum. Things have changed and, as Whitaker points out, 'Each change and expansion brings new dimensions of complexity in which uncertainties are increased, confusions compounded and comforts compromised' (Whitaker, 2002 cited in Chandler, 2006). These feelings are experienced by many heads as their role changes.

In July 2006 Ofsted published *Extended Services in Schools and Children's Centres*, which shared the findings of their survey of the factors which contribute to effective provision of extended services. A key finding was, unsurprisingly, that strongly committed leaders and managers were the key factors in success (Ofsted, 2006). This view is reflected in recent research such as the Effective Provision of Pre-school Education project (Sylva *et al*, 2003; Siraj-Blatchford and Manni, 2007) and the writings of Rodd (2006), Whalley *et al* (2004) and Goleman (1998).

It is a great step forward to see children and their families as a priority within national debate and the impressive plans that exist to have high quality, joined-up services at national, local authority and community level are to be commended. However this step forward comes with dangers, for what works well as innovative one-off projects may be much harder to roll out across the whole country:

> Innovative projects are frequently developed by people with vision, inspiring leadership and unbounded energy – finding enough of them to run children's services throughout the country may be a challenge! (Pugh and Duffy, 2006:1)

Challenges and Issues

In many ways leadership in multi-agency settings such as children's centres should be quite straightforward. Our role is clear: we are here to improve the outcomes for all children, especially the most disadvantaged, and we know more about what helps to do this than ever before (Sylva *et al*, 2003). Guidance on leadership seems readily available, for example the DfES has produced the *Every Child Matters Toolbox for leading and managing multi-agency work* (DfES, 2005b) and the National College for School Leadership has developed the National Professional Qualification in Integrated Centre Leadership (NPQICL). So what makes it so difficult?

Leading in a multi-agency team offers a unique challenge, as it involves bringing together a range of services and professionals from different working backgrounds and actively promoting multi-agency working. To be a successful leader in a multi-agency team such as a children's centre requires the head to lead across professional boundaries.

There is a growing recognition that multi-agency teams, while having many benefits, are complex structures to lead and manage (DfES, 2004). Such settings seek to meet the wide-ranging needs of children and families, among them the most disadvantaged and excluded, through working with practitioners from a number of agencies in the maintained, voluntary and private sectors. Those leading in these settings are required to go where others have not gone before. Rodd has identified a further complication for leadership in early years settings:

> The reluctance of some early childhood professionals to identify with leadership aspects of their role stems from a lack of understanding of what leadership means in terms of an early childhood service. (Rodd, 1997:40)

In our experience there are seven key issues and challenges for those taking a lead in multi-agency teams. We would like to share them here.

Changing roles for heads and managers

Heads of children's centres and extended schools are unlikely to have direct experience of leading or managing all the services they are responsible for. Many heads of children's centres have previously been heads of nursery schools. While they generally have an excellent understanding of children's learning and development from three to five years and have successfully engaged parents in children's learning, they frequently have far less experience of running year-round extended services for children from birth. Neither do they have direct experience of running health or employment services. On the other hand those children's centre heads who have previously been Sure Start local programme managers have frequently developed excellent services for parents across a locality but may not have experienced the issues involved in running integrated education and care for young children.

The challenge is: can you effectively lead a service if you do not understand it deeply? Can one person lead on all this work by themselves? In short we argue that the answer has to be no. We need multi-disciplinary teams rather than multi-disciplinary practitioners. Being a head of a multi-agency team requires new leadership approaches, such as distributive and sustainable leadership, which offer opportunities for leadership to be shared amongst teams. It requires heads of centres to be confident in their own area of expertise, secure in their abilities as head, and open to the contribution of others. Being a head in such circumstances requires a shift in thinking. It means moving from models of headship where the head is seen as a charismatic leader – or sometimes a benign dictator – in charge of all that happens. Rather we need a model where the head holds the vision developed by all those involved in the centre's work, establishes a clear direction for the centre's development and is able to support others in achieving it, sometimes directly through staff employed by the centre/school and sometimes through a Service Level Agreement (SLA).

Developing leadership across the centre team

Developing and sharing leadership across a multi-agency team is a new area of work for many heads of centres and schools. Leadership is now shared with governors, a senior leadership and a middle leadership team. Children and parents as well as all members of the staff team have an essential role in developing the centre's work. The leadership team may include people directly line managed by the head and people from agencies with an SLA to provide some of the extended services for the centre or school.

This model of leadership often involves staff across the centre developing new skills and redefining their role in terms of leadership. For many staff, especially team leaders, it can mean a change from acting as a good role model for colleagues to taking a key role in areas such as curriculum development and performance management. While many are excited by the new challenges, for others the changes may lead to anxiety and stress. Whether the feelings are of excitement or anxiety, all staff need support and training to help them into their new leadership role. Governing bodies can also require help in moving to a new role. They are now required to take an active role in the centre's or school's development and to be able to hold the staff to account. Being able to support the centre staff but also to challenge them when necessary requires confidence, knowledge and expertise. Many governing bodies and management committees are confident in their role of supporting staff but require help to develop their role in challenging in a way that is constructive and helps to move the centre forward.

Bringing teams together

Developing children's centres involves changes for everyone in the team. Bringing together practitioners from a range of professional backgrounds to form a new team is a challenge. It is even more of a challenge when bringing the new team together involves established teams, for example combining staff from a nursery school, voluntary nursery or Sure Start programme. In such circumstances it is easy for parts of the team to feel taken over rather than merged. The amalgamation is likely to involve abandoning or at the least reassessing ways of working. It may well involve changes in job descriptions and terms and conditions. Leading a team forward when there is an often understandable nostalgia for the past requires sensitivity and the ability to enthuse and re focus. It requires creativity to help the team to make new connections and embrace the future.

Working with different terms and conditions

Another element in bringing the multi-agency team together is to develop, often at some speed, a shared understanding of the contribution of all the practitioners in the team, including those who do not have formal qualifications. Different pay structure and terms and conditions can give the impression that some roles are more valuable than others and lead to a sense of unfairness. Most multi-agency teams work within nationally agreed employment frameworks and it can take a great deal of resourcefulness to ensure that these are respected while ensuring that all practitioners feel that their particular role is valued.

Differing priorities

Children's centres and extended schools have an ambitious agenda and at times it can appear that the different strands of work conflict. For example, most practitioners would stress the importance of continuity and consistency for young children in order to ensure that positive outcomes are achieved. This priority can be in conflict with requests for flexible attendance for parents who are working or studying. While flexibility and responsiveness to individual families' needs is important, too much variation in hours/days of attendance can be confusing for the child and affect their outcomes.

Staff in multi-agency teams are often seconded from their home agencies rather than employed by the centre or school. This can lead to divided priorities: are they there to promote the priorities of their home agency or those of the children's centre? There can also be tension between offering a universal service to the community and prioritising targeted services to meet the needs of families deemed to be in need, for example because of issues around parenting skills or mental health. Targeting may appear to be a good way of getting resources to those who need them most. However, in our experience, people do not like to feel targeted, especially when they believe the targeting is because they are seen to have failed in some way. Offering the specific support needed in a way that does not label is best done in the context of universal services, where all families have access to services, and additional support is sensitively given as and when needed.

Time

Multi-agency working takes time. Teams need time to come together to develop a shared vision and understanding of their various roles and contributions. When a number of agencies are working with an individual child or family, time is needed to ensure the work is co-ordinated and each contri-

111

bution is focused. However, in our experience you can easily end up spending more time in meetings discussing the services to be delivered than in delivering them. It is easy to create 'collaborative inertia' in which the process of integration gets in the way of effective service delivery (DfES, 2005b).

Listening to stakeholders

Ofsted has found that the most effective providers of extended services ensured that there was time to develop services in response to what the community said it wanted and needed (Ofsted, 2006). Listening to stakeholders is essential, but there can be a dilemma when what stakeholders are saying they want for their community does not match with the agenda the children's centre or school is required to deliver. For instance, providing full day care is a key part of the children's centre agenda. Yet many centres have found that a good many parents in their community do not want full day care but would prefer part time provision. Being faithful to the principle of listening and responding to parents, while at the same time implementing centrally agreed decisions, can present challenges.

Leadership teams in children's centres and extended schools need to develop new skills and understandings. What each team needs to develop will depend on their previous experience, but may well include skills such as managing fees and multiple use of premises, as well as skills in managing a change process. It is not enough that the leadership team knows what the centre or school is trying to achieve: it is also essential that they know how to achieve this.

Thomas Coram Centre for Children and Families

At Thomas Coram we have encountered many of the challenges identified above. In this section we share where we are now and something of the journey. This is not a list of ten top tips for running a successful multi-agency team but we hope that an insight into our work will be helpful to others on the journey. While there have been services for children on our campus since the eighteenth century, this section focuses on our development as a children centre over the last few years.

About the centre

Thomas Coram Centre for Children and Families is situated in Camden, London and is part of the Coram Community Campus. The centre is a partnership between Camden Local Authority and Coram Family. It was one of the first centres to be designated as a Sure Start children's centre and has school status. The community the centre serves is one of economic, cultural, linguistic and religious diversity. It is one of the most deprived wards in the country, and 20% of the children who come to the nursery are referred via the 'safeguarding children' panel.

The children's centre consists of:

- the nursery, providing inclusive, integrated education and care for 116 children from aged six months to five years 48 weeks of the year. We also have a childminder network attached.

- the parents' centre, providing drop-ins and crèches for children, individual and group support for parents, specialist groups including young parents, English as an additional language, fathers and male carers, parents who have children with special needs; and adult training.

- the locality team for the Kings Cross/Holborn area, providing home visiting and outreach, health services, and training and employment opportunities.

Leadership

Each of the services listed above has its own head and currently eighty plus staff work as part of the children's centre. The complexity and range of services our centre provides would make it very difficult for one person to have the knowledge and expertise to ensure that every aspect of the centre's work is addressed in depth. The head of the nursery acts as children's centre head, co-ordinating the centre's development and ensuring that the steps needed to address the priorities identified are taken. With the head of the parents' centre and locality team manager, she makes connections between each service, so that children and families can benefit from joined-up working. Inevitably there are times when differences of opinion arise, and working with difference is an important part of leadership in a multi-agency centre. Our strategy is to return to the vision, aims and agreed priorities for the centre and use these to decide the best course of action.

Camden local authority has overall responsibility for the implementation of children's centres across the authority (Childcare Act, 2006) and holds the government funding for the centres. We link closely with officers responsible for this work to make sure that what we are developing at community level links to Camden's plans for the whole authority.

In the nursery, the senior leadership team includes the deputy head, who is responsible for inclusion, families and community, and who is the key to strong links across the centre and with outside agencies. The team also includes the assistant head, who is responsible for children's well-being in the nursery. This is a vital role. We are taking responsibility for children from six months old to five years old, for up to ten hours per day, 48 weeks of the year. We must ensure that we get it right for them. The positive impact of high quality provision in the early years is well researched; what is also well known is the negative impact of poor quality provision. So we must do all we can to ensure that children have the best start. The middle leadership team consists of the team leaders for each age phase, who also have responsibility for a particular area of learning across the centre. All members of the leadership teams have explicit and defined responsibilities that contribute to the effective running of the centre. It is essential that everyone upholds the vision and aims of the children's centre and the more they do this the more effective we can be.

Governance

Thomas Coram Children's Centre has a joint governing body. It consists of representatives of all those who have a stake in the centre's work: parents, practitioners, local councillors, a senior social worker, senior health visitor, voluntary sector providers, key groups in the local community and the nearby Institute of Education. As the governing body is constituted as a school governing body and has a clear legal status, it is able to manage a budget delegated and devolved by the local authority. There is an SLA between the governing body and the local authority outlining the services the authority will fund and the centre will provide. Some of the children's centre services are provided by agreement with other agencies and the governing body does not hold the budget but does have a monitoring role, to ensure that the extended services offered improve outcomes for children. The governing body has established four committees, each taking responsibility for different aspects of the centre's work: children and curriculum, parents and community, staff and training, finance and premises. All the committees have strong parental input and include practitioners from across the children's centre.

Working together

Developing the children's centre at Thomas Coram has entailed bringing together staff teams from the maintained and voluntary sectors. It has involved practitioners from education, care, health, community, voluntary and housing services in developing a way of working as a whole centre team. This has not been without challenges. One of the first tasks was to integrate the teams from a community nursery and nursery school, each with a clear identity and established ways of working. Developing philosophy and practice for a new centre while still acknowledging the work of the previous nurseries required sensitivity and a clear sense of direction. Since then the nursery has developed ways of working with colleagues in the parents' centre, who are employed by the charity Coram Family, and most recently with colleagues who had been part of the Sure Start local programme. The addition of new staff teams has meant revisiting ways of working, assessing them to see if they will still work in the new structure, and developing new ways of working. With eighty-plus staff such discussions can be lively and require staff to be confident in their own area of expertise and to value the contribution of others. It is important that all staff feel part of the children's centre, but with a large team and wide range of services this can be difficult. We strive to keep a balance between everyone knowing enough about what is going on across the centre to feel part of its development, and each member of staff having the time they need to focus on their particular contribution.

Developing a vision

A clear, shared vision for the children's centre has been a key element in developing our work together. The vision has been developed over time during inset training days and centre meetings. It was necessary to bring together the whole team to create the vision which has subsequently been adopted by all those involved in the centre's work. This has contributed to our having a clearer sense of our individual roles within the children's centre, and helps us to focus on the outcomes we want to achieve. Our agreed aim is to support, educate and care for children and their families in our community and through this to help them realise their potential and so enrich their lives.

Developing the vision and aims statement was an important starting point, but finding ways to translate the words into actions and the actions into better outcomes for children is the real work of the centre. We have done this by auditing our work as a centre against our vision and aims. These audits include contributions from children, parents, staff and governors. Through this process we have identified what we already have in place and the actions we need to take to improve. These actions have been prioritised in a three-year centre development plan and the different strands in the plan each have an implementation plan attached, outlining the tasks to be undertaken, the resources needed, the key individuals who will implement the plan and the successes we hope to achieve. Each implementation plan is the responsibility of one of the governing body committees. Progress towards the success criteria is monitored during monthly meetings of the heads of the three services and with the chair and vice chair of governors. Weekly senior and middle team leadership meetings and monthly whole centre meetings are used to ensure that every one is aware of what is going on across the centre and to undertake some of the tasks we have identified as needing input across teams.

Successful leadership of multi-agency teams

The initial start up guidance for children's centres identified the following aspects as being key to successful multi-agency working:

- Developing a shared philosophy, vision and principles of working with children and families at all levels and by all partners
- Ensuring a perception by users of cohesive and comprehensive services
- All members of the staff team sharing an identity, purpose and common working practices
- A strong commitment by all partners to fund and facilitate the development and delivery of integrated services. (DfES, 2003)

Developing these aspects needs effective leadership. An effective leader in a multi-agency team needs characteristics such as creativity, reflection, self motivation, highly developed social skills, being ethical, being passionate and a commitment not only to their learning but also to other people.

There is still a tendency to believe that there are some individuals who are born with the qualities that could make them effective leaders, while the rest are destined to be followers. We would argue that we all have the potential to be leaders (Whalley *et al*, 2004). Experience of doing it and the confidence that generates contribute to becoming a successful leader.

As we argued earlier, the model of leadership required in a multi-disciplinary team is not that of the leader whom others follow. Rather it is a model of leadership focused on how well the leader articulates, shares the vision and distributes the leadership to produce the desired outcomes. It is about a developing a team who lead change and influence learning (Ireson, 2005):

> Leadership in the early childhood field appears to be more about the result of groups of people who work together to influence and inspire each other rather than the efforts of one single person who focuses on getting the job done.' (Rodd, 1998:4; see also Worsley, chapter 8)

Multi-agency teams need effective management as well as good leadership. Management is an integral part of leadership. Leadership is essential to ensure a strong ethical underpinning for the centre's work and a clear value base. If the organisation is to run smoothly, however, good management structures and systems also need to be in place (see also Whitmarsh, chapter 5, on ethical practice). Management without leadership can lead to a mechanistic delivery of services and organisations (Chandler, 2006). But without effective management, leadership becomes unachievable.

Throughout this chapter we have stressed the importance of a shared vision and in our experience the simpler the vision the better. Developing a vision is about being able to do 'big picture thinking' (Goleman, 1998, see also Needham, chapter 4). The vision and aims need to be remembered by all those involved in the centre, so that they can inform day to day decisions. This can only happen if they are simple and clear. Pages full of vision and mission statements accompanied by lists of aims and objectives look impressive but too often remain in a file, unread and ignored.

Whilst creating a vision is very important, being able to implement the vision and see it realised is even more important. Effective leadership in multi-agency teams is about being able to identify goals, break them down into targets and make them achievable for the team. Explicit plans help participants perceive their role in terms of improving outcomes for children rather than according to their professional background (Siraj-Blatchford and Manni, 2007).

Conclusion

There are almost as many models of multi-agency teams as there are children's centres and extended schools, and each will have its own particular challenges. Developing and maintaining multi-agency teams can be demanding, and at times the focus can end up being on structures and systems rather than on the reason for multi-agency work. Multi-agency work is not an end in itself; it is a means to an end. It is vital to ensure that the focus for centres and schools is always on improving outcomes for children.

Ofsted has found major benefits from offering extended services in centres and school. Children's and adults' self confidence has improved and more positive attitudes towards what they can achieve have developed (Ofsted, 2006). By bringing services together we can make significant changes in the lives of children and families.

Being a leader in a multi-agency team offers a unique opportunity to develop and support leadership not only in colleagues but in children and parents. With the expansion of the Every Child Matters agenda there is a growing need for effective and empowering leadership that acts as an advocate for children in the early years and all who are involved with them. Current leaders in multi-agency teams have the valuable task of acting as role models for future leaders as well as ensuring the well being of children. Leadership in multi-agency teams is about a journey of discovery and learning: enjoy the journey!

Reflective task

1. How might the transition to multi-disciplinary working be a smooth process?

2. Consider the qualities of existing teams. How might these qualities be communicated and integrated into the new multi-disciplinary team?

3. How might all staff gain the leadership qualities required for successful multi-disciplinary team working?

4. How might the vision be translated into reality?

References

Chandler, T (2006) 'Working in Multi disciplinary Teams' in Pugh, G and Duffy, B (Eds) *Contemporary Issues in the Early Years (fourth edition)*. London: Sage Publications

Department for Education and Skills (DfES) (2003) *Children's Centres – Developing Integrated Services for Young Children and their Families. Start up Guidance* February 2003. London: Sure Start Unit

Department for Education and Skills (DfES) (2004) *Every Child Matters – Change for Children*. Nottingham: DfES Publications

Department for Education and Skills (DfES) (2005a) *Sure Start Children's Centre Start Up Guidance.* London: DfES

Department for Education and Skills (DfES) (2005b) *Multi-agency toolkit* http//:www.everychildmatters.gov/deliveringservices/multiagencyworking

Goleman, D (1998) What Makes a Leader? *Harvard Business Review*. November/December, p93-102

HM Treasury (HMT) (2004) *Choice for Parents, the Best Start for Children: a 10 year strategy.* London: HMSO

House of Commons (2006) *Childcare Act 2006*. London: HMSO

Office for Standards in Education (Ofsted) (2005) *Self Evaluation Form for Schools* London: Ofsted

Office for Standards in Education (Ofsted) (2006) *Extended services in schools and children's centres* London: Ofsted

Ireson, J (2004) *Distributed Leadership... the only way to go.* National College of School Leadership. http//:www.ncsl.org.uk

Pugh, G and Duffy, B (Eds) (2006) *Contemporary Issues in the Early Years (fourth edition)* London: Sage Publications

Rodd, J (1997) Learning to develop as leaders: perceptions of early childhood professionals, *Early Years,* 18 (1), 24-34

Rodd, J. (1998) *Leadership in Early Childhood* (second edition). Berkshire: Open University Press

Rodd, J. (2006) *Leadership in Early Childhood* (third edition). Berkshire: Open University Press

Siraj-Blatchford, I and Manni, L. (2007) *Effective Leadership in the Early Years Sector (ELEYS) study.* London, Institute of Education

Sylva, K, Melhuish, E, Sammons, P, Siraj-Blatchford, I, Taggart, B and Elliott, K (2003) *The Effective Provision of Pre-school Education (EPPE) Project: Findings from the Pre-school Period – Summary of Findings.* London: Institute of Education, University of London

Whalley, M., Whitaker, P. Fletcher, C., Thorpe, S., John, K. and Leisten, R. (2004) National Professional Qualification in Integrated Centre Leadership (NPQICL) Study programme, Book

Whalley, M. (2005), National Professional Qualification in Integrated Centre Leadership Rollout Training Guidance

Whitaker, P. (2002) Designing and Developing Integrated Services for Children and Families. Conference Paper. Corby: Pen Green Centre

7

Investigating the practical challenges of integrated multi-agency work

Faye Stanley

Many early years services in England are reviewing and evolving their practice in response to the shift in multi-agency awareness and government policy regarding children in their early years (Pugh, 2006). The notion of extended schools and children's centres acting as the hub of a community may require early years practitioners to work in new ways. All services operating in the early years sector are now required to have a shared vision of the developmental needs of children in their care that should also encompass the needs of the community in which the children are located. So professionals in the field are required to work as part of a co-ordinated multi-disciplinary team addressing the needs of children in a holistic way.

This chapter reports upon existing published research highlighting the strengths and challenges of multi-agency working. These benefits and challenges encountered by practitioners have been explored by interviewing staff in the field and visiting settings at different stages of the development of their multi-disciplinary practice. It was discovered that although practitioners welcomed the new ideology of multi-disciplinary working and realised that it was paramount in enhancing the developmental needs of children, particularly through the key worker approach, the breaking down of barriers between some early years professionals sometimes proved problematic and many of the benefits of multi-disciplinary working appear challenging in light of current practice.

Meeting the needs of children: the challenges for practitioners

In recent years the Government has invested much interest and financial support in developing multi-agency services for children and their families (Anning, 2005; Pugh, 2006). Many early years professionals have broadly welcomed this. They would agree that 'for too long, children's services have been narrowly conceived, compartmentalised and fragmented, focusing on one need or providing one function in isolation addressing one item on the agenda of one agency' (Wigfall and Moss, 2001, p1). The move towards integrated education, care and family support services has been supported by several research perspectives investigating the connections between practice and outcomes for children (Sylva *et al*, 2003).

This chapter examines some of these research perspectives and then investigates practitioners' responses to the multi-agency agenda. The results of a small scale study involving three interviews are used to show how managers and practitioners in two children's centres and a Special School view multi-agency working. This highlights some of the changes that settings may need to consider in order to achieve the benefits to children identified in the first half of the chapter.

The benefits of integrated centres and multi-agency working

I begin by outlining some of the key research which indicates that multi-agency work can benefit children. This research will be used to identify and explore two key areas where multi-agency approaches have been demonstrated to be beneficial. The first of these shows how improved information sharing can benefit children in terms of early identification, complementary services and value added support. The second area demonstrates the impact on the child of attending to family circumstances.

The Effective Provision of Pre-school Education Project (EPPE), a longitudinal study that has followed the progress of 3000 children in 141 pre-schools, demonstrated that improved educational outcomes at Key Stage 1 can be influenced by pre-school experiences and that in settings where children are part of joined-up thinking and multi-disciplinary working, they will receive a higher quality of care and learning experiences (Sylva *et al*, 2003). EPPE has also concluded that children make better intellectual progress in fully integrated centres and nursery schools, and these provide higher quality pre-school provision (Sylva *et al*, 2003). The quality settings projected warmth and were more responsive to the individual needs of the children. And the children showed better social and behavioural outcomes as well as greater intellectual progress and attainment at entry to school (Sylva *et al*, 2003). At the

Thomas Coram Early Excellence Centre, for example, which in 2003 became one of the first children's centres, children and their families are offered a one-stop shop for high quality, open access services in a deprived area of London (Coram Family, 2006). Services provided include day care, specialist support for children with special needs and a Listening to Children project. Health and Social Services also offer a child psychology service, social work support and speech therapy, and have close links with the Child Development Team. There are also parent groups and courses, childminding courses, a multi-agency training base for parents and professionals and creative art work-shops (Pugh, 2006). The Centre illustrates the benefits of a joined-up approach and has provided a template for the development of similar services in deprived areas elsewhere. While EPPE is perhaps the most influential research on the positive benefit of integrated centres, it must be remembered that many of the integrated centres that were part of the EPPE study were Early Excellence Centres, so were well funded, resourced and staffed. We therefore need to look for further models of multi-agency approaches to confirm their efficacy.

The Sure Start Children's Centre programme is based on the concept that providing integrated education, care, family support and health services is a key factor in determining positive outcomes for children and their parents. It has been greatly influenced by the EPPE findings (Sylva *et al*, 2003; see also Siraj-Blatchford chapter 1). The DfES (2006) has cited several case studies which have also highlighted the benefits of multi-disciplinary working in creating a family-centred and ecological approach. One example is of school staff working with child and adolescent mental health services (CAMHS), where the joint work has been identified as enhancing the children's happiness and well being. And in healthcare, Sloper (2004) (in DfES, 2006) points to multi-agency working that has been associated with better patient outcomes and lower levels of stress for the staff. The multi-agency 'On Track' programme was identified by NFER (2004) (in DfES, 2006) as having a positive impact on children and families at a relatively early stage. Families have also reported seeing improvements in their child's behaviour, becoming more involved in their children's learning and finding it easier to take up employment due to the provision of affordable childcare. (DfES, 2006). In support of this, part of Sure Start core activities is to implement schemes for family learning, raising parents' expectations and providing support services (DfES, 2005).

Professional training

A second key finding of the EPPE study was that the higher staff qualifications the better the educational outcomes for children (Sylva *et al*, 2003). As well as EPPE, research evidence from longitudinal studies in the USA (Schweinhart, 2005) and New Zealand (Wylie, 2003) also suggest that mixed pedagogies that combine child-initiated activities, supportive, responsive and engaged adults, together with developmentally appropriate adult-directed teaching, and involve parents effectively, greatly enhance the educational, economic, social and health outcomes for children.

Building on such findings on multi-agency working, the Government has introduced several initiatives to encourage and support professionals in developing greater shared knowledge and a shared language of child development and pedagogy. In 2006 *The Early Years Professional Standards* were produced (CWDC, 2006), setting out training routes which aim to develop a world class workforce to improve outcomes for children. The proposals suggest that Early Years Professionals will lead practice across the Early Years Foundation Stage (EYFS), to support and mentor other practitioners and model the skills and behaviours that safeguard and promote positive outcomes for children.

Sharing expertise on meeting the needs of children

It seems clear that the sharing of different professionals' thoughts, as well as benefiting the child directly, will help inform and develop professional practice. Different agencies such as speech and language therapists, psychologists, health visitors, nurses, play workers and academics all have an important role to play in advising and supporting each other on meeting children's individual needs. They can learn from one another. For example a speech and language therapist will offer excellent insight into particular strategies that can be used to support a child's communication skills, while a psychologist will give an alternative view on how this may affect a child or their behaviour. A play worker may make additional recommendations which will support the child further. Each complements the other's knowledge and area of expertise. If the logic of this argument in so clear, why then is multi-agency working viewed as such a challenge that it requires national interventions to promote it?

Anning (2005, p21) raises three issues that may be problematic in carrying out a family-centred approach on a practical level. She asserts that the values and beliefs of practitioners delivering such services may be in conflict with those receiving them. In addition, service providers' professional values and beliefs on the needs of children may differ between different disciplines. Finally, providers may find themselves trapped between meeting the needs of children and their families, and meeting targets set by the government. It is also advocated by DfES (2006) that when completing the Common Assessment Framework, key workers should be aware that the families themselves may have differing views on the needs of the child. We can, therefore, conclude that crossing professional boundaries and creating a family-centred approach based upon the needs of children may be problematic, particularly as early years professionals have received different training, knowledge and experiences, so will have different views of the needs of children.

The Common Assessment Framework (CAF) has clearly been developed with the sharing of expertise in mind and is a more standardised approach to assessing a child's or young person's needs for services (DfES, 2006). More importantly, the CAF has been developed for practitioners in all agencies to enable them to communicate and work together more effectively. As the DfES states, 'it is a tool to support practice... communication should not end with the completion and forwarding of the common assessment' (DfES, 2006, p2). It also advocates that the CAF should look at the child as a whole person and take into consideration the strengths as well as the needs of individual children. The CAF is therefore particularly important in a multi-agency context when addressing a range of needs: these require input from a range of practitioners who need a common understanding of the issues they are working to address (DfES, 2006).

Involving parents and addressing families

Weinberger *et al* (2005), reporting research based evaluation in a particular Sure Start area, have shown that children's emotional well being can be improved when risk factors, in particular family-based adversities, are reduced during a child's earliest years and protective factors which provide support are increased. They also report that health visitors working with Sure Start at a local level have developed many initiatives such as joint visits, sleep clinics, play and stay sessions, nutritional work and exercise classes. Education services in the same area have introduced community teachers whose role includes supporting transitions, quality assurance, training and ongoing support for providers and pedagogical modelling. What all these examples illuminate, is a variety of service providers all drawing attention to the needs of children and the importance of enhancing and nurturing these needs during the first five years (Weinberger *et al*, 2005).

As *Every Child Matters: Change for Children* (DfES, 2004) is further implemented under the 'five outcomes' for learning, services will be teaming up in new ways and children and young people will have far more to say about issues that affect them. According to the Children Act (2004), a key feature of an integrated service or centre is that it acts as a hub for the community, supporting children and their families. The Act suggests that this will be implemented through children's centres and schools where the sharing of information will primarily be distributed between early years professionals. It also proposes that the benefits of joined-up thinking will provide an opportunity to address a full range of issues around children's health and well being.

According to Edwards (2005, p4), multi-agency working needs to enable 'a responsive tying of protective factors around vulnerable children, young people and their families, while building their capacity to take control over their own lives.' Edwards suggests that through the key worker approach, practitioners should be following the child's trajectory, with a focus on the whole child and 'knot working.' The concept of 'knot working' was coined by Engestrom *et al*, (1999) (in Edwards, 2005, p3) and is defined as, 'a tying and untying of threads of support from different agencies around a child or family in response to interpretations of their needs and strengths when they need them.' This is significant when considered in conjunction with Every Child Matters policy, since it suggests a model where the educare centre becomes much more the hub of co-ordinated support than was previously the case.

Such change may represent a key change in role for many early educare settings (see Duffy and Marshall, chapter 6). Edwards advises that if we are to take advantage of multi-disciplinary working, we must see other professionals in the field as resources to build upon in our understanding of the child. This would develop over time with a building of relations and mutual respect. Edwards (2005, p4) uses the term 'co-construction of services' which involves, 'the tying and untying of support and an ability to not only articulate what you are doing, but also to be able to interpret and act on the messages given by service users with the users.' This appears to be a positive way forward, but also very challenging as practitioners embrace new roles and responsibilities. Such co-construction may involve following children across a variety of service provision to give everybody involved a shared understanding of each child.

The idea of a key person is paramount to supporting and making decisions about the level of support for each individual and is manifest in the CAF (DfES, 2006). From interviewing practitioners in the field it became apparent that the sharing of information was a benefit of multi-disciplinary working. It was pointed out that all services were based in the local area or on one site, which meant that professionals could 'draw on the talents of other people' and that 'experts are under one roof'. It was also reported that children in need were being referred much more quickly because of other professionals being on hand, and that good services resulted. This concurs with findings from Atkinson *et al*'s (2002) study on commonly identified outcomes of multi-agency work (DfES, 2006).

Children's centres' core services involve working with the child, family and community and developing links with other service providers and schools. As Browne *et al* (2002, p2) suggest, the goal of most of these collaborative initiatives is to improve child outcomes, recognising that many of the child's needs are closely linked to the needs of the family and community. Atkinson *et al*, 2002 (in DfES, 2005) also identifies some of the benefits of multi-agency working which include access to services not previously available, children's needs being addressed more appropriately and improved educational attainment and better engagement with education. This was echoed in the interviews undertaken for this chapter.

The case studies

Three exploratory case studies were undertaken, using semi-structured interviews with three practitioners involved in working as part of multi-disciplinary teams. The case study approach allows the researcher to get close to the subject of interest, partly by access to factors such as the practitioners' thoughts, feelings and desires, as well as their interpretations of everyday practice (Hitchcock and Hughes, 2003). The studies aim to analyse and explore practitioners' views on the needs of children and the benefits and challenges of working as part of a multi-disciplinary team to meet these needs. As MacNaughton *et al* (2001) point out, interviews allow case study researchers to explore the meanings that lie behind observed behaviours or documentary evidence. The interviews also allowed some exploration of issues that might emerge in other settings and present resistance to the development of multi-agency working. The interviews present responses that may, therefore, be helpful to other practitioners in the process of developing their multi-disciplinary roles. They highlight shared concerns and reflections on the effectiveness of developing strategies. Informal observations were also carried out in each centre to establish the services that were on offer, the layout of the building and the general working atmosphere among practitioners.

The case studies were chosen to reflect different stages in the move towards implementing multi-disciplinary work. The settings differ greatly in their context and aims. One of the sample was a children's centre manager working in a purpose-built children's centre which had been open for a year. Her role includes developing and providing integrated services to families through a multi-professional team. The second participant was a deputy manager and teacher of an up and coming children's centre for Sure Start, due to open in 2007. Her role includes being an advisory teacher for schools, a line manager for early years workers, advising on the setting up of a neighbourhood nursery, planning for 'stay and plays' and the general day-to-day running of the centre. The third participant worked in a special school with children who have physical disabilities. Her role includes class teaching, personal development of the children, extending ways to help children communicate and liaising with a variety of multi-skilled professionals in meeting the needs of the children on a daily basis. The interviewees have all been in their current role for two to four years. All stated that they had been working as part of a multi-disciplinary team since they began their current role.

The challenges that practitioners face in meeting the needs of children and how these might be reduced

As Edwards (2005) suggested, crossing professional boundaries was clearly an issue of concern for the practitioners, as staff have been trained in different ways and may have had differing experiences and values concerning the needs of children:

> Sarah: I recently contacted a social worker, as I was concerned about a particular child. She informed me that the issue I had discussed was not in any way high risk and that I should continue to monitor her. I felt disheartened, as I wanted reassurance that she was okay and that her basic needs were being met... Her views and feelings towards children seemed to be completely different to mine.

This practitioner was seeking reassurance that the child's basic needs were being met but the social worker also needed to be aware of the learning needs of the child and how this was affecting the child on a daily basis. It is interesting that she felt uncomfortable about crossing the boundary between her and the social worker and say that she needed this reassurance. This illustrates the insecurity sometimes felt in multi-agency partnerships over knowing what is appropriate to expect someone from a different discipline to do. Practitioners need to be prepared to ask for what they feel they need in order to support the child, and to negotiate new requests from partners. Simple as it sounds, cutting through interpersonal, social and cultural barriers to create a climate where people feel able to talk openly remains one of the biggest challenges of multi-agency working. Although in this example the child in question appeared not to be at immediate risk, it might have been an opportunity for the professionals concerned to come together and share their expertise and to look at the situation as a whole to decide if any further action was needed. The CAF may be useful in creating the points of discussion and documentation that could help pull services together by helping different service providers to meet to discuss their roles in meeting the needs of the child. Similarly another interviewer reported:

> Lisa: Professionals get stuck in their own practice, and are not willing to open up. This is proving problematic for us as not all the services are on one site; so breaking down barriers is proving to be difficult. We are finding that the barriers are slowly starting to break down, although it is an ongoing process. I have turned up for several joint meetings where the same professionals do not turn up. We view others as knowledgeable and [being] people we can draw upon as we are all in the job to meet the needs of the children. Unfortunately we do not always feel everybody shares this view.

Lisa is identifying a recurring challenge of multi-disciplinary working, observed when visiting several settings. Her final sentence indicates that while this early years provider feels that she values the input of other professionals, she does not feel equally valued. This is a message that is frequently conveyed by early years practitioners: that they feel undervalued. There may be various reasons for this relating to the training and seniority of those coming to case conferences, and also to the taken-for-granted role of early education. Whatever the cause, it is clearly an important element of partnership working that people all need to feel equally respected. They need to see that they are being kept informed by colleagues as a matter of course, and not as an afterthought. They need to attend meetings and send apologies for absence or lateness. Every practitioner needs to feel that their views are respected and that people have an understanding of what they can offer. The degree of communication will vary between settings. Some have service providers on one site while others may have no direct contact with other professionals due to their location.

The introduction of a common core of training for all professionals entering early years services is an important step. Everyone involved in the sector needs to support the development of initial and in-service training that helps to develop some common understanding of what the different partners can offer, better insight into their values and aims, and a common language for discussing children and families. It is hoped that this will give professionals a shared vision on the services they are providing and the principles that underpin them. A shared training framework will strengthen staff knowledge of child development, care and pedagogy, fostering continuity and progression. Lisa's comment below illustrates how barriers may be reinforced by initial difficulties and emphasises the importance of co-ordinated and collaborative steps forward:

> Once established, multi-disciplinary working will be much easier as everybody will be pulling together... however it is frustrating when people don't. It is hard to establish.

At a centre or setting level, it is therefore essential that practitioners make their beliefs explicit and reflect upon the service they are themselves providing (Anning, 2005). Policy documents could be written for parents and partner agencies, as well as for internal staff and inspectors. It would involve all the professionals working as part of a particular setting or centre, for example health visitors, early years workers, midwives, speech and language therapists, family officers, nurses, occupational therapists and psychologists. Reviewing policy documents with external partners will help keep these up to date and relevant and offer a forum for developing shared practice, and it will encourage practitioners to cross professional boundaries. Such an approach requires staff time to observe and talk to the children about their experiences, what they like or dislike about a service, finding out the needs of the whole child and therefore ensuring that services wrap around their needs.

Louise spoke about addressing family circumstances in a broader context rather than focusing upon the child alone:

> In our children's centre we get parents to fill in questionnaires and ask them their current views on services they receive and what they would like to receive. We act on as many as we can. For example, we have recently introduced a crèche in the afternoons as well as the mornings as parents felt that this would be more suitable. Some parents also highlighted that they felt there should be a group for dads, which we are also beginning to implement.

This setting in particular regularly consulted parents or gave out question-naires for them to have a say in what they wanted from their setting. Parents were also offered sessions such as computer classes and behaviour manage-ment. The key worker would liaise so that all the agencies involved could meet together to discuss their child's needs. However, evidence from these three case studies suggests that in addressing family circumstances, there is still a long way to go.

Common themes from the three centres

This chapter has demonstrated that while meeting individual children's needs by adopting a broader focus on family can be effective, practitioners are faced with genuine challenges in achieving such a focus. The benefits of multi-disciplinary working and the notion of joined-up thinking have been welcomed by many early years professionals. There is also common agree-ment in each of the settings researched, based upon the ecological model of Bronfenbrenner (1979), that the characteristics of the child, the family and the society within which they live, have a significant impact upon a child's development, and that a change or conflict in one of these areas will have a ripple effect upon the child and their developmental progress.

The importance of a key worker approach in aiding the tying and untying of services around the needs of the child has been a common theme throughout the research literature and appears to be at the forefront of providing high quality early years services. This must be viewed as a positive step forward in ensuring better protection and earlier intervention for our youngest children. Other benefits identified in multi-disciplinary working involve the cross fertilisation between the different agencies. Many practitioners value the opportunity to take a holistic approach to the needs of children. This was identified in all the interviewees' responses. It was also noted that there should be quicker and easier referrals for children to services or expertise.

Many of the benefits of multi-disciplinary working were also deemed to be challenges. For example, some of the challenges in multi-disciplinary work-ing include the different beliefs, values, knowledge and experiences of early years professionals, and the difficulty that some are unwilling to cross profes-sional boundaries. As Edwards (2005, p4) states, 'If we are to take advantage of multi-agency working we need to think systematically and see other pro-fessionals as resources to be drawn on in our focus on the child or young person... equally we will be seen as resources for others'.

In relation to sharing expertise, while it is agreed that all staff need to have a common core of training, as in Sweden and in Reggio Emilia in Italy, there is also need for greater equity amongst early years professionals and their roles (Fabian and Dunlop, 2002), and for the development of shared values through shared activity. Each team member needs to have sufficient knowledge of all the services on offer and a shared vision, so the service can be used to its full potential, and parents and children can receive continuity and progression. This presents a special challenge in a country where early years provision is so diverse, and where it may therefore be inevitable that the ethos and approach of various early years settings will differ.

Reflective task

- ■ Draw a diagram to show the connections to one of the settings mentioned in this chapter and other agencies.

- ■ Compare this to a diagrams devised by you to illustrate the connections to a setting you know or to the case study in chapter one.

- ■ Highlight what you think are the strengths and weaknesses in different colours.

- ■ Consider what steps might be taken to address the weaknesses.

References

Anning, A. (2005) Investigating the Impact of Working in Multi-Agency Service Delivery Settings in the UK on Early Years Practitioners' Beliefs and Practices. *Early Childhood Research* 3 (1) pp19-50

Atkinson, M., Wilkin, A., Stott, A., Doherty, P. and Kinder, K. (2002) *Multi-agency working: A detailed study* Slough: NFER

Bronfenbrenner, U. (1979) *The Ecology of Human Development. Experiments by nature and design.* Cambridge, MA: Harvard University Press

Browne, E.G., Amwake, C., Speth, T. and Scott-Little, C. (2002) The Continuity Framework: A Tool for Building Home, School and Community Partnerships. *Early Childhood Research Practice* 4(2) pp1-18

Children's Workforce Development Council (2006) *Children's Workforce Development Council Homepage* http://www.cwdcouncil.org.uk

Coram Family (2006) *Coram Community Campus* http//:www.coram.org.uk

Department for Education and Skills (DfES) (2004) *Every Child Matters* http://www.dfes.gov.uk

Department for Education and Skills (DfES) (2005) Sure Start Children's Centres: Practice Guidance http://www.surestart.gov.uk

Department for Education and Skills (DfES) (2006) *Benefits of Multi-agency Working/ Common Assessment Framework.* www.everychildmatters.gov.uk accessed 9/7/06

Edwards, A. (2005) *Ne-cf Conference papers* http//:www.ne-cf.org/conferences

Fabian, H. and Dunlop, A.W. (2002) *Transitions in the Early Years.* London: Routledge

Hitchcock, G. and Hughes, D. (2003) *Research and the Teacher*. London: Routledge

MacNaughton, G., Rolfe, S.A. and Siraj-Blatchford, I (2001) *Doing Early Childhood Research*. Maidenhead: Open University Press

Pugh, G. (2006) *Contemporary Issues in Early Years (fourth edition)*. London: Paul Chapman

Schweinhart, L. (2005) T*he High/Scope Perry pre-school study through to age 40. Summary, conclusions and frequently asked questions.* Ypsilianti: High/Scope Press

Sylva, K, Mellhuish, E, Sammons, P, Siraj-Blatchford, I, Taggart, B and Elliot, K (2003) *The Effective Provision of Pre-School Education (EPPE) Project. Findings from the Pre School Period* http//:www.ioe.ac.uk/projects/eppe

Weinberger, J., Pickstone, C. and Hannon, P. (2005) *Learning from Sure Start*. Maidenhead: Open University Press

Wigfall, V and Moss, P (2001) *More than the sum of its Parts? A study of multi-agency child care network*. London: National Children's Bureau

Wylie, C. and Thompson, J. (2003) The Long-term Contribution of Early Childhood Education to Children's Performance-Evidence from New Zealand. *International Journal of Early Childhood Education* Vol 11(1) 69-78 March 2003

8

Exploring the perspectives of early years practitioners in a newly established children's centre

Jenny Worsley

This chapter focuses on the practical implications of multi-disciplinary working and includes a case study of a children's centre to explore the perceptions and experiences of early years practitioners and service managers in developing a multi-disciplinary approach. This discussion is informed by learning organisation theory and, in particular, Wenger's studies of communities of practice, to propose a tentative model of practice aimed at how multi-disciplinary collaboration can be achieved. Changes to cultures of practice are an integral part of the reform of children's services. Lave and Wenger's (1992) model will enable practitioners to reflect on the nature of the culture being created in their particular setting.

The case study centre is located in an inner city area and is evolving out of a local Sure Start programme. The staff has recently relocated to a large purpose-built building, offering a range of childcare services including a neighbourhood nursery, playgroup and crèche. Health professionals and family support workers are also on site and future initiatives involve organising employment advice sessions and providing training courses for parents. Liaison with local schools and a family centre complement the services available. Informal open-ended interviews were undertaken with the programme manager and early years co-ordinator to obtain data relating to their experiences of providing joined-up services, in the hope of providing useful insights of work currently being undertaken and identify some of the concerns and areas of good practice when developing a multi-disciplinary approach.

Current initiatives

Early years services are undoubtedly undergoing far-reaching and challenging changes in light of national and local policy initiatives prompted by *Every Child Matters* and the subsequent *Children's Workforce Strategy* that 'will require the workforce itself to become more integrated and more flexible' (DfES, 2005 p33). The intention of these reforms is to establish a more cohesive, diverse and adaptable early years workforce. This requires collaborative and outward looking ways of working, not just within children's centres but also increasingly within local networks of services. By bringing together a range of professionals from different backgrounds, including health, education, employment advice and family support in conjunction with settings, the ideals of multi-disciplinary work, and joined-up services, involving the development of multi-professional relationships and nurturance of parental involvement, are proposed as part of an evolving culture of practice.

The workforce strategy recognises that a highly qualified early years workforce leads to improved quality provision. The Effective Provision of Pre-School Education Project (EPPE) (Sylva *et al*, 2004) found that settings that have staff with higher qualifications improve the quality of provision offered – with improved outcomes for young children. This links to there being informed knowledge of child development, recognition of the important role of parents, the ability to develop effective relationships with young children and the provision of 'instructive learning environments' (*op cit*). This implies that new and existing early years practitioners need to develop their skills and knowledge by undertaking further training and qualifications. As Fleet and Patterson (2001) suggest, in a climate of philosophical and pedagogical challenges, it is valuable to recognise the importance and complexity of developing professionalism within the context of early years education and care. Their research into the professional development of early years practitioners concludes that although dissatisfaction with current practices and feelings of disheartenment due to low status and pay were evident, there also existed 'a climate of intellectual inquisitiveness' (*ibid*, p2).

According to O'Keefe and Tait (2004, p37) the growth in higher education institutions offering early childhood studies degrees, and the development of part-time foundation degrees in Early Years is a move by the Government to enable early years practitioners to develop their skills and knowledge and provides an opportunity 'to think abstractly and consider the relativism of the multi-faceted and super-complexities of their role'. Such courses will hopefully support practitioners in developing a flexible attitude to their work with young children and families and ultimately to develop more effective methods of working within multi-disciplinary teams. As Edwards (1999 p1) argues, the emergence of new early years professionals will require expertise and confidence in working across different 'professional cultures of health care, nursery nursing, social work, voluntary work and education'. However, meeting these challenges may not be easy. Indeed, the workforce strategy itself acknowledges the difficulties that may arise:

> We are looking to overcome the restrictive impact that professional and organisational boundaries can have so that increasingly professionals and practitioners from different sectors work better together in multi-disciplinary teams around the needs of children and young people and share an increasingly common language and understanding. (DfES, 2005, p3)

Multi-disciplinary working

Crucially, the rhetoric recognises 'the restrictive impact' of professional boundaries that exists between the different agencies, although one of the challenges in meeting government policy is that there are very few models for setting up and managing joined-up services and multi-disciplinary working practices, or available training or guidance on how it can be achieved (Anning, 2005). This is a view echoed by Warmington *et al* (2004, p1), who argue that current policy on joined-up working is 'running ahead of the conceptualisations of inter-agency collaboration and learning required to effect new forms of practice'. If multi-disciplinary approaches are to be achieved, early years practitioners should not be left to falter when putting policy into practice. As Lumsden (2005, p40) observes: 'for students and practitioners in the early years this is an exciting and challenging time as the importance of government policy that involves joined-up thinking and collaborative action becomes integral for improved outcomes for all children'.

Several questions arise. What are the implications for early years practitioners of translating policy into practice? How does this differ from current practice? Is there a gap between existing provision and that envisaged for the future? When considering these questions and thinking about new ways forward, it is useful to look at the forms of multi-disciplinary working already being undertaken.

The Sure Start model of integrated services to achieve better outcomes for young children and families within their local communities offers scope to develop the proposed children's centres. The on-going evaluation of Sure Start programmes may give some useful insights in relation to barriers to effective practice and similarly the opportunity to highlight successes. Equally, a recent study of early excellent centres by Anning (2005) has provided an overview of the challenges facing early years practitioners in developing an integrated services approach. One of the key outcomes identified by the evaluation is linked to the management of staff from different services and the importance of providing support and training for managers. The difficulties of meeting the needs of diverse staff, including training, developing confidence, and determining how collaborative work is established and extended, have also been identified (Campbell, 2003).

The ideal of multi-disciplinary work is not new, and Jenny French has explored the historical origins of the term in chapter three. However, a reminder of the implications of multi-disciplinary work for early years practitioners may be useful. Edwards (2004) argues that the new forms of multi-disciplinary working being promoted differ significantly from previous versions such as 'partnership working' where there was limited sharing of goals or working practices, or from 'locating services together' without joint goals, or from 'the development of an all purpose standard multi-agency professional', none of which are in line with current thinking. Edwards (2004) acknowledges that individual practitioners will face new demands, but she argues that this should not equate with the erosion of professional identity; rather it should involve increasing one's current knowledge and being willing to share it with others.

Research for NFER by Atkinson *et al* (2005) identified five models of multi-agency activity. In the 'centre-based delivery' model, a variety of agencies are drawn together in one place to offer more co-ordinated and wide-ranging services. A second, 'co-ordinated delivery' model involves a number of agencies in the delivery of services, to enable a more cohesive response to need. It appears that these two models offer an insight into expectations of how multi-disciplinary work is to be achieved in children's centres. However these are broad models and what also needs to be recognised is that different modes of inter-agency working within children's centres will be required, depending on the needs of the local community, resources and funding. It is not enough to locate services together; there needs to be the ability to work and communicate across professional boundaries, an acceptance of different ways of working, the adoption of joint goals, and development of shared understandings of what other professionals have to offer (Edwards, 2004). The research by Atkinson *et al* (2005) provides useful findings relating to the numerous challenges of multi-disciplinary working and identified several practical issues:

- Roles and responsibilities – increased work and pressure, under-standing of their personal role and the role of other professionals, understanding the constraints of other agencies

- Communication – at all levels of working, especially day-to-day communication, information sharing, consultation

- Conflicting professional and agency cultures – different policies and procedures, ensuring agency commitment, appointment of staff, the establishment of common aims and objectives, personal com-mitment, sharing funding and resources

These are by no means the only issues, but the areas highlighted identify the kinds of challenges inherent in multi-disciplinary working. It is important these issues are acknowledged if we are going to avoid difficulties in the pro-cess.

Collaborative activity and communities of practice

There has been an attempt to provide an overview of the current agenda relating to children's services and some of the issues relating to the develop-ment of a multi-disciplinary approach. The theme of collaboration between the different services is embedded within the Government's ideas of multi-disciplinary work. However definitions of this term are broad. Rodd (1998, p185) refers to the importance of 'transforming traditional power relation-ships into collaborative, consultative, communicative, respectful decision-making.' Any organisation is by definition a collective, consisting of indivi-duals with differing views and beliefs communicated through their own per-spectives. The belief that individuals do not work and learn in isolation has been highlighted by Easterby-Smith and Araujo (1999, p5) who showed that 'the more tacit and 'embodied' forms of learning, involved situated practices, observation and emulation of skilled practitioners and socialisation into a community of practice'.

Lave and Wenger (2002) provide a useful framework for analysis of social learning in communities of practice, and the development of multi-discip-linary work within a children's centre can be linked to this development of a community. Individuals can be seen to unite together and hold each other answerable in terms of a collective understanding the community's core con-cerns. These are constructed through the establishment of joint aims and objectives, policies and procedures, and an understanding of their own and others' roles and responsibilities. Individuals also build and develop their community through reciprocal commitment, involving interaction to esta-blish meaningful relationships; for example, communicating through meetings and sharing information. Finally, communities of practice establish a shared repertoire of communal resources, for example, language, funding, procedures, and shared understanding of the constraints placed upon different agencies. Lave and Wenger (2002) suggest that the establishment of a successful community is reliant on several factors, including designing organisational structures that recognise the importance of informal learning, recognising the importance of participation and communication, and developing methods of linking different communities together through shared dialogues and co-ordination of different practices.

In the development of a community of practice within a children's centre, early years practitioners will have the opportunity to engage in mutual interactions, share their own professional knowledge with others and participate in a holistic approach (Lumsden, 2005) to working with young children and their families. Warmington (2004) acknowledges that the development of a community requires a high level of agreement among members in the formation and safeguarding of a shared vision of practice. It is important to acknowledge that this takes time and effort, and as Rodd (1998, p176) rightly suggests, 'early childhood professionals will require all their skills in communication and interpersonal relationships to build the cooperation of others'.

Organisational learning and the learning organisation

The projected centres will be dissimilar, 'reflecting differences in ideology, discipline, experience and knowledge between staff' (Melhuish, 2004, p3), but also in the expressed needs of the community they are offering services to. When commenting upon the development of a community model in Pen Green early years centre, Whalley (2001, p130) highlights the necessity of responding to continually changing needs and suggests that 'centres for early childhood with care should be learning organisations'.

Pedlar *et al* (1991, p3) defines a learning organisation as:

> A place where people continually expand their capacity to create the results they truly desire, where new and expansive patterns of thinking are nurtured, where collective aspiration is set free and where people are continually learning how to act together.

The idea of continuous professional learning is introduced and, as previously discussed, this links well with the ideals of multi-disciplinary work. As Edwards (2004, p5) rightly suggests:

Individual practitioners will certainly be facing new demands. These include professional multi-lingualism, fluid trusting inter-professional working, the capacity to make their expertise explicit, the negotiation of broad local alliances and the co-construction of provision with service users. The necessary learning will take time.

When discussing the establishment of a learning organisation, Cardno (2002, p211) suggests that the 'notion that learning is associated with change is by no means new', and further comments, 'what is new, is a renewed interest in the potential of facing up to learning that might be extremely difficult and

---

Table 1

Organisational learning

1. **Foundation**
   Basic skills development, plus encouraging learners to develop the behaviour and enthusiasm to learn more. Strategies to motivate and build confidence for further learning are used.

2. **Formation**
   The organisation encourages self-learning and reflective practice for self-development and enlightens individuals of their own role and responsibilities within the organisation. Training opportunities are made available to meet the demand for learning.

3. **Continuation**
   Innovative working practices are developed, learning needs become more individualised with more focused training opportunities.

Shift to a Learning Environment

4. **Transformation**
   A change in organisational culture, characterised by fairness, openness, flexibility and valuing people's efforts.

5. **Transfiguration**
   People are the primary concern of the organisation, where learning is at the centre of activities, professional credentials are low priority and the organisation is instructing and controlling itself by means of total involvement in the community. The organisation is judged by the extent to which people who make it up control and teach the organisation how to learn, rather than vice versa.

Adapted from Jones and Hendy, 1992 (in Keep and Rainbird, 2002)

---

disquieting'. Learning does involve change that can be very threatening and depends on 'practitioners altering their beliefs, adding to or changing their knowledge and revising their practices' (Edwards and Knight, 1994, p148). A five-stage model of development of a learning organisation is proposed by Jones and Hendy 1992 (see page 141). The first three stages link to organisational learning, while the final two stages represent a shift to a learning organisation.

The attainment of the 'transfiguration' stage equates to practitioners gaining a sense of control over their own learning and how this relates to organisational development. Louis *et al* (1996) (in Anning and Edwards, 1999) suggests four features of a learning organisation. The first of these requires that a shared sense of purpose prevails; however, this is reliant on exploring what this shared sense of purpose actually means and clarifying the practical implications to all those involved. In a children's centre, early years practitioners will need to discuss their aims in collaboration with other professionals to reach an agreement on the objectives underpinning the services offered. The second feature is that a collective focus on learning is inherent. This may relate not only to children's learning and wellbeing but also to professional development, by sharing expertise and gaining an understanding of others' roles and responsibilities, and this helps to ensure that collaborative activity is embedded in working practices. The third feature links to de-privatised activity and to the previous two aspects, where activities are observable. The emphasis on exploring each other's practice is necessary to help ensure that good use is made of existing skills within a new model of integrated services. The fourth feature proclaims the importance of reflective dialogues, where practitioners discuss and reflect on actions and share insights. The opportunity to participate in discussions relating to what has worked and what has not, exploring and interpreting it together, will foster understandings and develop the context of a community of practice. This is an important ingredient for enabling children's centres to adapt continually and meet the challenges of continual cultural change. For early years practitioners, it means taking a dynamic role in the development of services rather than taking a passive position by merely following directives (Rodd, 1998).

Case Study: Perceptions and experiences of learning and community

The idea of the organisation as a context for social learning was evident in the perceptions of the staff of the case study children's centre. Opportunities for training and development linked not only to individual needs but also at organisational and community level. The knowledge and skills of the more experienced staff was utilised to support newly qualified practitioners using informal learning. As the early years co-ordinator commented:

> Some of the staff may not have the skills as yet to be able to complete the common assessment framework and more senior staff would guide them at first until they were competent to do so.

Whilst training and development was recognised as a priority to ensure that the services offered were meeting the needs of children and the community, the early years co-ordinator recognised that changes were needed quickly, often before training courses were available. All those employed were qualified to a minimum of NVQ level 3, but the aim was for all workers eventually to achieve graduate status. This was perhaps a key point: it was considered that if early years practitioners were to meet the challenges of shifting their professional identities (Edwards, 2004), they would need the confidence, knowledge and skills to do so.

Example 1: Training and Development

Opportunities for training are available for all staff, not only short courses including behaviour management, counselling, child protection awareness, Birth to Three framework, Curriculum Foundation Stage, but through whole team training days and away days. Training is then disseminated by cascading information to colleagues through presentations at team and subgroup meetings. The sharing of information and raising awareness of each other's roles and responsibilities are the primary reasons for inter-agency training days.

Training is recognised as crucial for the development of effective services, but also for increasing staff confidence and skills. (Field notes, 2005)

Practitioners felt that the need to ensure that information was shared was an important factor. The interviews highlighted that the multi-agency subgroups provided an opportunity for professionals from all disciplines to become aware of the constraints that practitioners from differing agencies experienced, as well as knowledge of what they had to offer in the provision and development of services. It was also felt that the shared training with colleagues from health, family support services and education, and with parents, helped practitioners to be more open about their activity and enhance collaborative practice. These are key features in the development of a learning organisation as identified earlier in this discussion and could also be linked to the transfiguration stage of the model proposed by Jones and Hendy (1992), where learning is at the centre of the activities.

Example 2: Communication

Individual and joint team meetings are undertaken regularly to discuss issues pertinent to individual teams, such as early years services, health workers and family support. Subgroup meetings are then held, made up of representatives from respective teams and parents and local schools. Issues raised from both these meetings are discussed at board meetings, which include representatives from local schools, team members, parents and managers.

Consultation with parents and the community is undertaken continually, for example by using community focus groups to determine what the local needs are and how services should respond. To encourage attendance a £5 gift voucher has been offered as an incentive. (Field notes, 2005)

Developing communication and dialogue, both in formal team and committee meetings and informal brief conversations, enabled practitioners to discuss practices across agency boundaries. However, what must be recognised is that the development of reflective conversations will be a continual process, dependent upon the development of relationships and the willingness and confidence of the practitioners. According to Cardno (2002, p212), reflective practice and communication can be challenging, 'especially when problems have several dimensions and give rise to tensions between competing values and beliefs'. What is of value is that the opportunity for 'mutual engagement' existed and practitioners perceived it as an important requirement.

One of the key difficulties in managing integrated provision and multi-disciplinary working was outlined by the centre manager. Other agencies have their own priority targets which they are required to meet at the expense of the centre's targets. For example, family support workers managed the provision of a baby club but it was indicated that this service would have been more effective if health professionals were involved. Unfortunately, due to their workload and targets, they were unable to participate. This was overcome by recruiting early years professionals who had health related qualifications and experience. This demonstrates the importance of flexibility when providing an integrated approach by utilising the resources available. If the multi-dis-

Example 3: Integrated Provision

The centre has developed a range of integrated services; one such example is by working in partnership with family support services to offer mother and baby clinics and a baby club for parents/carers. Parent craft classes were also provided, as well as a playgroup three afternoons a week. A crèche room is available to give parents the opportunity to leave their children for a time – e.g a 'shopper's crèche' – and when parents were attending courses or support groups at the centre. The provision of childcare is seen as an integral service to enable parents to access the services and training courses available at the centre. Another successful area of provision is the development of on-site parental and adult training courses, including computing, literacy, numeracy and childcare. Opportunities for employment support and advice are also provided in workshops at the centre.

'Joined up working' is evident, with a number of professionals from different agencies sharing information, e.g. family support workers are notified by health professionals of children under 5 and families who would benefit from home visits, and support services offered by the centre. Early years practitioners extended their role, not just in providing care and education in the centre but also in outreach work, helping community groups to develop early year's provision and also working in and providing support and guidance to community playgroups. The centre staff work closely with a local family centre and are providing services previously under the umbrella of social services, such as 'stay and play' sessions, parent support classes. This helped to avoid duplication of services. (Field notes, 2005)

ciplinary working is to be achieved effectively, individual agency targets need to be integrated more effectively into shared targets.

Sloper (2004) suggests that there is very little evidence at present of how the ideals of multi-disciplinary working identified in the Every Child Matters agenda will help to realise improved outcomes for young children and their families. So it is important to evaluate current and emerging practices to help develop our knowledge of multi-disciplinary working and gain a sense of the changes that are required. It is hoped that this case study provides an insight into how one centre is managing new ways of working across disciplines. While the development of a range of integrated services was evident, including family learning, childcare facilities, employment services and community outreach work, the centre manager indicated that the provision of services was often dependent on the goodwill and enthusiasm of other professionals. The hope was expressed that as the Every Child Matters agenda becomes a statutory requirement, changes at organisational level will ensure that some of the barriers identified will diminish.

Conclusion

A model of practice development has been presented in this chapter that may be helpful to professionals developing a multi-disciplinary approach. A commitment to a shared vision, the development of a climate of trust and respect, and acknowledgement of the diversity of different professionals is required. For early years practitioners, this involves transcending the boundaries of care and education inherent in their profession, by 'understanding the implications of working in a multi-disciplinary context' and 'being focused on the child and not necessarily on [their own] professional practice and comfort zone' (Cozens, 2004, p30). The development of a community of practice and a learning community is explicitly linked to the ideals of government policy of multi-disciplinary work in children's centres. For early years practitioners, the opportunity to re-conceptualise their role through reflective work-based enquiry and critical thinking is highlighted within current literature as a positive feature in professional development. As Fleet and Patterson (2001, p11) observe:

> Work in the early childhood field is diverse and sophisticated; professional development opportunities for staff need to embrace complexity and move beyond narrowly focused instructional models of adult learning.

The social aspect of learning with and through others is a key feature in developing complexity: as suggested here, developing critical reflective practice is not a simple task, especially, perhaps, for inexperienced practitioners. Lave and Wenger (1992) believe that practitioners in any organisation are apprentice learners until they have developed a thorough understanding of what tasks are involved; only then do they become complete members of the community of practice. In the light of government expectations for the development of multi-disciplinary work, children's centres are an ideal context for practitioners to create and manage their own future, develop communities of practice, overcome cultural boundaries and generate a climate within the organisation where continuous learning is inherent.

The chapter has also highlighted exemplars of current practice and some of the barriers to multi-disciplinary working. It is difficult to judge whether these examples will be constructive as we move forward, but looking at existing methods gives us some idea. To judge from the perceptions and experiences of the practitioners, there is little doubt that what they have accomplished so far has been seen to be of value to the community as a whole in offering a more co-ordinated approach. We can see the willingness to communicate information, work with other professionals, overcome barriers by adapting practices, share training outcomes, and recognise the important contribution that young children and their families can make to the provision of services.

What is of concern is that government policy is perhaps exceeding guidance on how this can be achieved at a practical level. Lumsden (2005) rightly argues that an attractive ideology proposed by policy makers can disguise the underlying restrictive barriers, so that practitioners who have the responsibility of translating policy into practice may do little because they lack understanding. The rhetoric of multi-disciplinary work and joined-up thinking in the establishment of children's centres, combined with the introduction of the Foundation Stage for children aged 0-5yrs (2005) has re-conceptualised the role of early years practitioners. But there needs to be time for the consolidation of new knowledge and skills. Many practitioners will need support, guidance, training and advice on how to progress towards Early Years Professional (EYP) status, by receiving appropriate experiences and training.

Issues for reflection

■ Early years services are undergoing radical changes. Meeting the challenges of change and innovation and continuous evaluation of provision can be rather daunting in constantly changing environments and this needs to be considered. What strategies might a team develop to keep up to date with changes?

■ There is the expectation that early years practitioners will develop their expertise and skills to improve the quality of service, but to accomplish this staff will need to have appropriate support and training. Therefore such training should be available, and the design of courses should be flexible, especially for existing practitioners, as the balancing of employment, academic study and family commitments presents challenges. What practical steps can training agencies take to support people in their learning?

References

Anning, A. (2005) Investigating the impact of working in multi-agency service delivery settings in the UK on early years practitioners' beliefs and practices *Journal of Early Childhood Research,* Vol. 3, No.1, (pp.19-50)

Anning, A and Edwards, A. (1999) *Promoting Children's Learning from Birth to Five: Developing the new early years professional* Maidenhead: Open University press

Atkinson, M. Doherty, P. and Kinder, K. (2005) Multi-agency working: models, challenges and key factors for success *Journal of Early Childhood Research* Vol. 3, No.1 (pp.7-17)

Campbell, A. (2003) Developing and Evaluating Early Excellence Centres in the UK: some issues in promoting integrated and 'joined-up services *International Journal of Early Years Education* Vol. 11, No. 3, October 2003

Cardno, C. (2002) Team learning: opportunities and challenges for school leaders *School Leadership and Management* Vol.22, No.2 (pp.211-223)

Cozens, A. (2004) Taking the Green Paper from Vision to Reality. Paper delivered at NCEF 2004, Association of Directors of Social Services. NCEF conference centre

Department for Education and Skills (DfES) (2005) *Children's Workforce Strategy* London: DfES Publications

Easterby-Smith, M. and Burgoyne, J. and Araujo, L. (1999) (Eds.) *Organisational Learning and the Learning Organisation* London: Sage

Edwards, A. (2004) Multi-agency working for prevention for children and families: 'It's the biggest change since the introduction of the NHS. Paper delivered at NECF 2004, Birmingham University. NECF conference centre

Edwards, A. and Knight, P. (1994) *Effective Early Years Education* Buckingham: Open University Press

Fleet, A. and Patterson, A. (2001) Professional Growth Reconceptualized: Early Childhood Staff Searching for Meaning *Early Childhood Research and Practice* Autumn 2001, Vol.3, No. 2 (pp.1-14)

Jones, A. and Hendry, C. (1992) *The Learning Organisation* Bromley: HRD Partnership

Keep, E. and Rainbird, H. (2002) Towards the learning organization? Cited in Reeve, F. Cartwright, M. and Edwards, R. (2002) (Eds.) *Supporting Lifelong Learning* London: RoutledgeFalmer

Lave, J. and Wenger, E. (2002) Legitimate peripheral participation in communities of practice. Cited in Harrison, R. Reeve, F. Hanson, A. and Clarke, J. (2002) (Eds.) *Supporting Lifelong Learning: volume one* London: RoutlegeFalmer

Lave, J. and Wenger, E. (1992) *Situated Learning: Legitimate peripheral participation* Cambridge: Cambridge University Press

Lumsden, E. (2005) Joined up thinking in practice: an exploration of professional collaboration. Cited in Waller, T. (2005) *An Introduction to Early Childhood: A multi-disciplinary approach* London: Paul Chapman Publishing

Melhuish, E. (2004) *Presentation from the National Evaluation of Surestart. Paper delivered at NECF 2004*, Executive Director of NESS. NECF conference centre.

O'Keefe, J. and Tait, K. (2004) An examination of the UK Early Years Foundation Degree and the evolution of Senior Practitioners – enhancing work-based practice by engaging in reflective and critical thinking *International Journal of Early Years Education* Vol. 12, No.1 (pp25-42)

Pedlar, M., Burgoyne, J., and Boydell, T. (1991) *The Learning Company* Maidenhead: Mcgraw Hill

Rodd, J. (1998) *Leadership in Early Childhood: The pathway to professionalism* (2nd Ed.) Buckingham: Open University Press

Sloper, P. (2004) Facilitators and Barriers for co-ordinated multi-agency services *Child: Care, Health and Development* Vol.30, No.6. (pp571-580)

Sylva, K. Melhuish, E., Summons, P., Siraj-Blatchford, I. and Taggart, B. (2004) *Technical Paper Twelve: The Final Report* London: DfES/Institute of Education, University of London

Sylva, K., Sammons, P., Melhuish, E., Siraj-Blatchford, I. and Taggart, B. (1999) *Technical Paper One: An Introduction to the EPPE project* London: London Institute of Education

Waller, T. (2005) *An Introduction to Early Childhood: A multi-disciplinary approach* London: Paul Chapman Publishing

Warmington, P. (2004) Conceptualising professional learning for multi-agency working and user engagement. Paper delivered at the BERA 2004, University of Birmingham.

Whalley, M. (2001) Working as a Team. Cited in Pugh, G. (2001) (Ed.) Contemporary *Issues in the Early Years: working collaboratively for children* (3rd Ed.) London: Sage

9

Collaboration with parents:
the role of the multi-agency setting
in working with parents

Karen Clarke and Amanda French

Families are the main context of learning for most people. Learning within the family is usually more lasting and influential than any other. Family life provides a foundation and context for all learning.

Riches beyond price: making the most of family learning, NIACE (1995)

Background

The Government's Green Paper *Every Child Matters* (HMSO, 2003) set out its vision of how society should be organising itself to meet the needs of all children. The evolution of children's centres and extended schools and the kinds of multi-agency working which they promote, promise a more holistic approach to meeting the needs of children and families. In educational terms they also provide an ideal opportunity to work collaboratively with parents on their own learning and that of their children. This will, hopefully, mean that a range of family needs can be met through links to childcare and education provision. *Every Child Matters* acknowledges the need for a clear commitment to working with parents and carers as an essential part of working with children. This has clear implications for the educational development of families coming into contact with the multi-agency settings. It is also important that the full range of family involvement with children is recognised through the opportunities on offer. This should include family friends, step-parents and other members of 'blended' families such as step-siblings, non-resident parents, grandparents and foster parents. Opportunities also need to be accessible for families which have members with particular needs such as learning and mental health difficulties and disabilities.

This chapter explores the different ways in which all parents and carers can be fully involved in the educational services offered by multi-agency sites such as children's centres and extended schools. It also examines the concept that multi-agency working is an ideal medium for promoting collaborative practices with parents around their own and their children's learning across various educational contexts.

What is family learning?

Family learning incorporates infinite variations on formal and informal learning that involves more than one generation of family members. It covers a wide range of models such as the now well-established Story Sack and Babies into Books initiatives as well as one-off, broadly educational events held in libraries, museums and galleries. There is also the range of courses funded by the Learning and Skills Council (LSC) with adult education, further education and community education providers. Family learning is often embedded into other programmes such as parenting skills, family support and home-school initiatives. There is often confusion about what the term actually means. The LSC uses two main categories to distinguish the work it funds: Family Literacy, Language and Numeracy programmes (FLLN) and Wider Family Learning (WFL). These terms have been increasingly used by other agencies such as the National Institute of Adult and Community Education (NIACE) and the Department for Education and Skills (DfES) to discuss and describe their work in this area. Accordingly they are the terms that we will be using throughout this chapter.

For information, the DfES and LSC have put together a list of fundable family learning programmes in their publication *Family Literacy, Language and Numeracy: a guide for policy makers* (DfES, 2004b).

New initiatives in family learning included a national two-year initiative called Skills for Families, which was rolled out across seventeen LEA partnerships from 2003/4. This is designed to embed FLLN across a range of programmes, train practitioners and develop further resources as part of the wider Skills for Life agenda. Development for wider family learning programmes is not so closely tied in to government strategic thinking on education; however, it is acknowledged that it contributes to many other community projects such as community capacity building and neighbourhood renewal. Provision for families is part of the adult and community learning offered through local authorities. In 2004/5 £11 million was made available for wider family learning programmes. Given the current financial restrictions on adult education, this indicates the extent to which family learning is seen as an important lever for widening participation in adult learning generally. Widening participation in learning is also part of the Government's agenda for expanding the workforce, both in the field of childcare and through the Basic Skills Programme.

Renewed interest in family learning

Family learning is not a new concept and there is a long tradition of providing many different, often very innovative forms of family learning, some of it pioneered by independent charities organisations such as the Workers Educational Association and Barnardo's, on which new initiatives such as Sure Start can and have drawn. And long before the recent government policy, many informal family learning opportunities were established in some playgroups, schools, early years settings, libraries and adult education and community centres. However, the opportunity for the expansion of a more integrated approach to family learning is now a reality, due to the development of multi-agency environments such as children's centres and extended schools. Family learning programmes are already established in many Sure Start programmes and many feature strongly in the Early Excellence Centres. Children learning along with their parents or other adults in a familial relationship can make a positive difference to the lives of the children and their parents (Siraj-Blatchford and Clarke, 2000). These new multi-disciplinary settings allow the integration of family learning into other kinds of support and learning opportunities for families by bringing the expertise of so many kinds of professional knowledge together under than one roof.

The Green Paper *Every Child Matters* (HMSO, 2003) acknowledges the need for a clear commitment to working with parents and carers and recognises and supports the important role they inevitably play in their children's experiences of learning. There is a large body of research that indicates the numerous ways in which the home setting is an important and powerful source of learning. Multi-agency working needs to encourage and enable all families to facilitate and support their children's learning. This is part of what Bronfenbrenner (1979) has referred to as a mapping of the child's ecosystem. Policy-makers and professionals increasingly regard home and school, parents and practitioners as having similar functions in raising children and so needing to work in partnership (Alexander 1997). Parents are expected to do more than give their children love, intimacy, security, and safety; they are expected to stimulate their children's intellectual development and be actively involved in their school careers (Lareau, 1989). Lareau also identifies wide social differences in parents' abilities to work in partnership with professionals to support their children's learning. Some parents find it difficult, requiring staff to be encouraging and sensitive so they can enable parent partnerships to grow and thrive.

In terms of *Every Child Matters* (DfES, 2004), most family learning provision falls within the remit of 'universal services', which is the only place it is mentioned in the Green Paper. Outside of this proposed 'universal' provision some Family Language, Literacy and Numeracy (FLNN) will be targeted at specific schools or areas where there is much educational disadvantage and low achievement, whilst other learning provision is specifically aimed at children with particular learning needs such as speech and language therapy. Other targeted provision is designed to meet the needs of particular groups in the community such as refugees and asylum seekers.

Recent research (Siraj-Blatchford and Clarke, 2000) and current government policies (HMSO, 2004) clearly recognise that there has always been important learning taking place in the home at both pre-school and school-age stages in a child's life. The home-based period of a child's early learning, the way a mother or any primary carer communicates with her child is a crucial component in the preparation of the child for lifelong learning (Siraj-Blatchford and Clarke, 2000). Atkin and Bastiani (1988) examined how parents think about teaching and found that, not surprisingly, they understand education as being about a range of roles, tasks and approaches. At one end of the spectrum, this includes parents working with their children on activities which are intended to achieve specific outcomes, usually using explicitly educational materials in formal settings. At the other end, there is a more informal approach where the parent or carer seeks to support and motivate the child through shared attitudes and a range of activities, most of which are not explicitly educational. In the former approach, the teaching content or educational outcomes are perceived as the most important aspect of the activity, whereas in the latter, it is the process of learning that takes centre stage.

The pertinent point here is that these approaches to teaching and learning can be replicated with parents and children in multi-agency working in early years settings. How familiar children and parents are with such approaches may determine whether they participate in them outside the home. Bearing this in mind while looking at the ways in which parents or primary carers interact with their children in the home, can be useful in shaping family learning provision in early years settings. Provision can thus complement existing patterns of learning and teaching and can also introduce adults and children to new ways of learning.

Family learning covers many different areas. Whilst it can be and often is about the roles, relationships and responsibilities of family life and supporting children, FLLN can also include learning basic skills such as literacy and numeracy that will help them support their children's learning in school. In addition, there is growing interest in providing family learning opportunities that help family members relate to a concept of a wider society in which the family is a basic building block for citizenship, thus contributing to the development of a cohesive social fabric (NIACE, 1995). These include programmes designed to give adults the confidence and skills to join community groups such as tenants' associations and school boards of governors. Little concrete research has been done on how effective these programmes are in increasing such involvement; however anecdotal evidence would seem to suggest they at least pave the way.

Current policy and government initiatives

The Sure Start initiative, which began in 2000, represents a serious attempt by the government to eradicate child poverty. Sure Start programmes were established in disadvantaged areas in England and Wales. Each programme had weekly targets that were specific to the needs of that area, in addition to the longer-term objectives set out by the government. The Sure Start programmes have been evaluated over the last five years and further funding has been secured to ensure sustainability (NESS, 2002). Sure Start has changed over the last five years but has been able to continue with some of its key features. Some of the characteristics of Sure Start have also been incorporated into the Green Paper *Every Child Matters* (DfES, 2004) and also into recent legislation in the Children Act (2004). Indeed, the concepts of promoting social and emotional development, improving health, improving children's ability to learn and strengthening families and communities lie at the heart of recent government initiatives. Children's centres and extended schools aim to continue the work started for young children and their families in disadvantaged areas to include all children and their families and provide multi-agency services under one roof. Many early years establishments have already secured a firm basis for working with parents and families. This has taken the form of both formal and informal learning.

Case Study

One nursery that has forged positive links with the parents and the local community is Ogley Hay Nursery School in the West Midlands. This nursery school, which, incidentally, wished its name to be acknowledged in this example of good practice, is described as having 'significant levels of deprivation within the local community. Approximately one quarter of the children have special educational needs, which is above the average' (Ofsted, 2001, p7). The constructive ways developed by the staff for working with parents meets the criterion of 'ongoing dialogue' (*Every Child Matters*, 2004, p28).

Informal 'conversations with a purpose' (Burgess, cited in Mason, 2002, p62) were conducted with two parents and four members of staff to elicit information about the inclusion and partnership aspects of working with parents. Discussions with the staff focused on ways of enabling parents to feel they were a part of their children's nursery education.

I invited the parents in to the coffee mornings, then they got involved with the story sacks. This moved on to them helping the nursery staff such as laminating and help with promotional events.

(Nursery nurse with responsibility for parents' groups, December 2005)

In the first place we went to the library because they were offering free computer courses that I knew some of the parents were interested in. When I was there I joined in and as I didn't know how to use the computers I was the same as the parents... we got chatting and then the parents started to want to stay at the nursery when they brought their children in.

(Nursery Nurse, December 2005)

These examples show the sensitivity needed for successful inclusion of parents and eventual partnership. They exemplify the respect and supportive attitude that staff should display to parents so that the interactions between all parties are constructive and valued (Dowling, 2005).

The discussions with the parents centred on what benefits they felt had accrued from working and interacting more closely with the staff. For two of the parents interviewed, the involvement with the nursery led to employment in the childcare field. This was partly because the local Early Years' Development Partnership had NVQ level 2 training in childcare as one of its targets and funded these initiatives. The training was delivered at the nursery – an example of joined-up thinking.

> I had no idea that when I first stared on the NVQ training that this would lead to the job I have. It is my dream job.
>
> (Family Worker who completed NVQ 2 and is undertaking NVQ Level 3, December 2005)

The funding for the family worker came through the Nursery Development Grant Scheme which, for this nursery, is going to be continued. This particular nursery school has been designated as a children's centre from 2006, and from 2007 will evolve as part of the extended school cluster with local primary schools.

> Coming here and doing courses but also doing things with my child raised my self-confidence... I had no qualifications but now I've got my NVQ 2 and I work as a classroom assistant... but it was really good, you know, fun to do, not like in a classroom when you were at school.
>
> (Classroom assistant/parent)

Istance *et al* (2002) explore the different ways in which family learning, amongst other community education initiatives, strengthens relationships in families and cuts across the generations, not least through the positive effects of improving communication skills and self-confidence. Clearly, children are likely to benefit from any improvements in their parents' confidence and self-esteem, not to mention the financial benefits gained from improved education, training and employment. However, in addition to the kinds of social capital benefits outlined by Schuler (2002), the political pay-off for many of these initiatives is reduced dependency on state benefits. Many parents, especially mothers, find their first engagement with adult education a crucial step back into the workforce. Thus a commitment to increasing opportunities for parents to learn can be seen as a means of enhancing the economy (Penn,

2005). This objective is reflected in other related initiatives (*Skills for Life Strategy*, 2001, *The Learning Age*, 1998)

> I started coming more to the nursery because I wanted to know more about the nursery. I came here ten years ago and I'm still coming! I've done lots of courses here that I would never have thought I would... like behaviour management. I've got my First Aid Certificate. I liked coming because it was friendly and you could, you know, discuss things and worries. I've also made a lot of friends.
>
> (Classroom and playgroup assistant, December 2005)

One of the key concepts of current policy is to reduce unemployment levels, even though they are at the lowest recorded (Brown, 2005). Thus, if parents are in employment, there is more of a chance of reducing the number of children who are living on or below the poverty line. However, for many parents, the goal of employment still, for various reasons, remains unachievable. The proposed children's centres will be to offer a range of additional services and would appear to be an ideal venue for providing educational benefits that will raise parents' expectations both for themselves and for their children.

> I think the big asset about becoming a Children's Centre and then part of the extended school will be that there will be additional funding so that we can offer more opportunities to the parents.
>
> (Head teacher of nursery school, December 2005)

> Before the nursery started having parents in, the only place I could meet anyone was down the shops and then you couldn't have a proper chat.
>
> (Parent from nursery school)

In addition to the discussions with parents and staff, narrative, naturalistic, non-participant observations were also undertaken to see the parents' involvement with their children's learning in action. An added bonus in these observations was seeing the interaction between staff and parents, which appeared to be an easy, tension-free relationship.

Parent: I think yours is better than mine – I like the angel wings.

Child (*aged 23 months*): wings face (*pointing to mother's card*)

Parent (*to member of staff*): I've never done anything else like this before I'm having such a good time.

Together the parent and child then walked around the room together showing other staff what had been achieved.

(Observation, December 2005, at the mother and toddler session at the nursery)

The enthusiasm shown by the parent who has made her own card with her own handprint had mother and child laughing together and commenting on each other's cards. The sense of achievement, coupled with the enjoyment of doing something together raises the self-esteem of both child and parent.

Mum: Like this (*holding hands under tap*) yes, that's good.

Child: Splash, plash, plash.

Mum: Splish, splash, now we can dry them.

Child: Dry, dry.

Nursery nurse: Now your hands are dry, we can see if your painting's dry too. Where's mum's painting? (*Child points to it*)

Mum: I didn't think he would know which was mine. Can I take mine home too when it is dry? I want to put them in a book I'm making for him.

(Observation of mother and child washing their hands after painting, mother and toddler group, December 2005)

This scenario illustrates a model of one of the five outcomes (making a positive contribution) from the Green Paper *Every Child Matters* being explicitly enacted in a naturalistic manner. The five outcomes detailed in this Paper offer opportunities for parental collaboration in the form of courses for themselves or involvement in their children's learning. The outcomes – being healthy, staying safe, enjoyment and achievement, making a positive contribution and achieving economic well being – are better accomplished when staff are aware of the value of parental involvement.

The concept of parents and families learning together is not new. There have been many initiatives in the past where early years establishments and schools have provided opportunities for learning together. Some of these have been very successful and have been discussed in an Ofsted survey of family learning which showed that 50% of adults who had taken part in a family learning activity went on to further training or education (Ofsted, 2000). The development of both extended schools and children's centres is intended to ensure that the needs of that particular community are fully identified and met. However, the provision of united services and purpose-built buildings does not automatically determine success. The success of any joint learning will depend on the ethos, the values and the commitment of the staff involved.

Previous initiatives for parents focused on parenting and skills for employment have not been entirely successful. One reason could be that tension exists between the ideas and principles held by professionals and those held by parents. The concept of multi-agency working is one of partnership, which implies a sharing of values and respect for all parties. It is this concept that needs to be extended to the parents if any headway is to be made in achieving the goals of tackling poverty (Pugh, 2001, p117) and achieving economic well being (*Every Child Matters*, 2004). However, partnerships need to be developed: they do not just occur. In order for true partnerships to develop, practitioners need support over the ways they can work with parents; they also need a pedagogy that recognises parental contributions to learning. The premise of this pedagogy is one that acknowledges and respects the parent-child relationship (Devereux and Miller, 2003).

Developing people and partnerships

The holistic approach suggested by an emphasis on multi-disciplinary working is not just about professionals working together more effectively. It should also involve an explicit recognition that support networks between parents, carers and professionals need to be established and maintained. These networks should not be conceived and treated as though they exist just to support parents in the traditional and rather patronising ways typical of the past, where the implication was often that parents were incapable of supporting themselves without professional intervention. Rather it should be acknowledged that such networks can be mutually supportive for professionals and parents alike. In a truly collaborative relationship, parents are just as likely to be able to support professionals in their work. If the collaboration is genuine, then community networks will help to maximise the effectiveness of children's centres and help develop meaningful working relationships between parents and professionals. However, collaboration relies on a number of critical factors: there must be real involvement in the curriculum planning for these joint learning activities; a shared understanding of the practices of each unit within the children's centres; mutual exchange of information and a common language, and respect for the values of all the parties concerned.

A crucial aspect to working in partnership with families is that of communication. In a multi-agency setting this is of vital importance. It is of even greater importance when working with families where 'them and us' barriers are easily created. Barriers between professionals and the families can exist for a variety of reasons (Taylor and Woods, 1998). The actual dialogue may be at an inappropriate level and professionals may impose their own set of values and beliefs on the families with whom they are working. When these barriers are apparent, collaboration, partnership, and therefore family learning, are ineffective. Hurst and Joseph, 1998, (cited in Nutbrown, Hannon and Morgan, 2005) argued for an understanding of 'the complex cultural differences and shifts which children, parents and practitioners experienced when they entered each other's worlds and opportunities for each to 'share' the other's' (*ibid* p13). The communication skills needed for successful collaboration have to be developed by both the practitioners and the families. Interaction and negotiation are a basic principle. Children's centres will need to provide opportunities for initial interaction with families that does not place pressure on anyone involved. This will require a co-ordinated effort on the part of all the professionals to ensure that there is understanding of the complex cultural differences.

Another key aspect is involvement. True collaboration means sharing in the decision-making process. Many parents feel that professionals are much better placed to make decisions about their children and are hesitant about voicing an opinion. It is the responsibility of staff in children's centres to ensure that parents' contributions are valued and acted upon in the right context. Sure Start ensured that parents' views were heard by including parents on its management committees – an example of good practice that should be followed by the management or steering committees of children's centres. Sure Start has commissioned evaluative research about the effectiveness of the programmes. Independent evaluation is important to identify, foster and extend good practice. This, again, is not a new concept: over twenty years ago Tizard and Hughes (1984) recognised that it was time to change the emphasis away from what parents should learn from professionals to what professionals could learn from parents. Many primary schools have adopted a more participatory style of management and have actively encouraged parental involvement with their children's education (Passey, 2000). This, again, has evolved from *Every Child Matters* and the new Ofsted framework that has been developed from the aims of this Green Paper. However, this partnership ideal has been slow to materialise in areas of social deprivation and areas where there is a wide cultural mix of people. Many parents from minority ethnic groups, and working-class or single parents, have difficulty coping with the material disadvantages they encounter so find it difficult to get involved with their children's education (Siraj-Blatchford and Clarke, 2000). This is, in part, because of the perceived power imbalance and what families perceive as tokenistic collaboration. For many families (Pugh, 2001), partnership with perceived professionals and educators is not a part of the culture.

I think it was because there was no pressure: you know, we asked parents to stay for coffee and biscuits when they dropped the children off in the morning: you know [the parents] did not have to go back and come out again. Also, I think it was the informality and relaxed atmosphere – you know – many of the parents had a bad experience in school and inviting them in like this helps to show that school is not a bad place.

(Comment from member of staff in nursery school when asked what she considered to be a successful strategy for working with parents, December 2005.)

This comment clearly demonstrates empathic understanding and sensitive awareness of the local community. Initially to capture the parents' participation in the nursery, there had to be a great deal of flexibility in the daily routine to accommodate this informal drop-in facility. The informal approach adopted by the nursery has clearly helped to break down perceived barriers and the kind of drop-in facility described could become part of the children's centre strategy, especially when a new build is in place. This non-didactic approach was highlighted in evaluative research carried out in Sheffield (Weinberger, Pickstone and Hannon, 2005). The other factors researched by this team were the need for sensitivity to local needs, and mutual support for all the people involved in these centres.

The evolution of children's centres offers to take the best from previous strategies, evaluate them and re-present them to complement twenty first century ideals.

One objective in the Sure Start programmes has been to strengthen families and communities, in particular building the community's capacity to sustain the programme and thereby create pathways out of poverty (Weinberger, Pickstone and Hannon, 2005). This notion has been incorporated into the manifesto for children's centres. In order to sustain the programme parents need to be involved at management and board levels. In addition to sensitivity about local needs, staff need to have excellent communication skills, and demonstrate these through negotiation skills and team building expertise. These skills are vital if parents are to be fully involved with the decision-making process, leadership and governance of the centres.

Research by Sylva and Siraj-Blatchford (1995) suggests that parents should be involved in the planning and implementation of the curriculum. Consequently, parents need to have precise information about such aspects as learning outcomes and how the children can achieve them. Once again, this information sharing needs to be done in a manner that is accessible to all, with translations where necessary and confidence building taken into account. There are other features about involvement to consider. Epstein and Brandt, 1991 (cited in Siraj-Blatchford and Clarke, 2000) indicate that there are five areas of parental involvement:

- parenting skills, child development and home environment for learning
- communications from school (establishment) to home
- parents as volunteers
- involvement in learning activities in the home
- decision-making, leadership and governance

The future for parent involvement
Siraj-Blatchford and Brooker (1998) set out a strategy for improving partnership with parents and families; this is summarised below. But success depends on the willingness of staff to acknowledge parents' values and beliefs, as well as the staff's commitment to accept changes that may be necessary within themselves. Additionally, staff need to demonstrate genuine empathy with and interest in the families so that knowledge can be shared in a non-threatening ambience.

Communication
Communication should be considered from various points of view. First, written communication: is it in community languages? Is it in plain English?

Are there some visual cues for parents who may have difficulty in reading? Secondly, oral communication: the tone of what is said can alter the perception of the listener. Is there training in basic counselling skills so that speakers are made aware not just of the content of what they say but also of the manner in which they say it? Finally, is there complete understanding between the speaker and listener?

Values and beliefs

It is easy to make assumptions about what other people believe, based on a person's own experiences. This is where equal opportunities training and awareness is beneficial. Awareness and knowledge of equal opportunities is an area that should receive regular review to keep practitioners abreast of changes in the diversity of the population. The diverse backgrounds and experiences within the local community are positive contributions to children's learning and to the life of a centre. The centre and the plethora of agencies working within it need to show that they are a part of the community; that the hopes and challenges of the community are interconnected to the centre.

The environment

The environment encompasses curriculum activities as well as the physical location of the centre. All staff will know about welcoming aspects of visual and informational material, but is there someone ready to talk to the parents without being rushed? Is there a space for the parents? Facilities in centres should be utilised to the best possible advantage and parents should be viewed as a high priority.

Pedagogy

A change in the curriculum is needed so that learning outside the educational establishment is recognised and valued. Parental and family contributions can then have as much value as formal learning. Although early years establishments follow the Foundation Stage Curriculum (FSC) many do not adapt to what the child may have learned in the informal setting of home within the learning goals of the FSC. This change in pedagogical approaches must evolve from all professionals involved with the child. For some, this may mean a massive shift in beliefs.

Quality audit

If areas of good practice are identified right away, staff will start the development of partnerships in a positive manner. These quality aspects can be extended to include parents' views about resource allocation and to contribute to the development plan. External reviewing of the provision together with action research can identify good practice as well as the areas that would benefit from change or improvement.

What exactly does the partnership entail?

As a starting point, staff should be clear about the extent of the partnership. Is it a peripheral one; do staff and or parents only meet briefly once or twice a week? Or is it fully inclusive? This may entail lengthy discussion and possibly a change of perspective.

Research has shown that fostering and sustaining the parent/centre partnership invariably benefits the staff, parents and, most importantly, the children's learning and development (Siraj-Blatchford and Clarke, 2000).

Critical analysis

One of the key aims of current policy (Blunkett, keynote speech, Learning Skills Council, 13 July 2005) is to reduce unemployment levels. The reasoning suggests that if parents are in employment, there is a greater chance of reducing the numbers of children living on or below the poverty line. This ideology clearly informs the other government initiatives discussed. The emphasis today in the UK is on reducing dependency on state benefits and getting people, especially mothers, back into the workforce as a means of enhancing the economy (Penn, 2005). So parents who would prefer to stay at home full-time are not a priority. Similarly, the linking of family learning to educational disadvantage could lead to a situation where it is perceived more as support for struggling parents than as learning in its own right for all families.

The proposed children's centres will offer a range of services and would appear to be an ideal venue for providing educational benefits that will raise parents' expectations for both themselves and their children. However, possible tensions between different groups of professionals and the families may inhibit the promotion of constructive partnerships.

Despite all the reported advantages of multi-agency working enhancing family learning, there are important issues to consider if growth is to be sustained. NIACE has argued for a national framework or strategy for family learning that would develop, promote and illustrate its multiple benefits and, not least, explicitly explore how they interact with various government policies. This stems from a wider lack of clarity about family learning at both policy and practitioner level. Principally this is about how the success of family learning is measured, which is problematic if there are no agreed criteria or specific targets.

Ideally, one could take the view that the developmental gains of adults and of children on family learning programmes are equally important and mutually inclusive and reinforcing.

Alternatively, one could argue that family learning is principally about addressing children's underachievement in school. In this sense pre-school and early years family learning could diminish social inequalities by helping parents become more informed about and involved with how their children learn. However, one could also argue that family learning in the school environment may overemphasise the children and parents and disregard other members of the family. In addition, there are parents with unhappy memories of their own schooldays who find the thought of attending family learning programmes in a school distasteful.

Lastly, there is the argument that family learning contributes to the whole nebulous concept of citizenship and stakeholder involvement in society at large. Whatever the conception of family learning is, the heart of the issue lies in true partnership and collaboration.

Questions arise about family learning services at local level. For instance, at present most existing provision rests within adult and community services: there are some family or early years services but provision of this kind is not consistent across regions. Moreover there is uncertainty in local authorities over where to locate family learning in the future, although this may be re-solved when all the new Directors of Children's services have been appointed.

The sector Skills Council for Children and Young People's services is charged with developing a workforce strategy for practitioners across the range of children's services. The government needs to think about how family learning practitioners will be included in such a strategy. The Qualifications and Curri-culum Authority (QCA, 2005) and the National Family Network have ap-proved a framework for national occupational standards for family learning practitioners. This all points to a clear workforce development issue.

A common core of training is proposed for those working in any capacity with young children, and the Early Years Professional Standards will provide a framework for it. Existing family learning tutors are not mentioned in the Green Paper, but in many areas tutors have established strong links with parents and families. They also have valuable expertise of working with both adults and children. A NIACE report on Family Learning (2003) expressed support for a national staff development strategy for practitioners working in FLNN and wider family learning. As with other workforce developments in early childhood settings, this would undoubtedly improve the standard of provision. There is also a clear need for transparent training routes and the recognition of prior learning and qualifications for both adult educational and early childhood practitioners.

Consequently, long-term strategic issues for family learning need to include greater coherence and co-operation between different agencies on a national and local level. In the light of current disappointing figures for adult participation in education, there is a need to harness the obvious popularity of family learning to help exploit all possible opportunities to re-engage adults in learning. This will promote more joint learning between parents and children. Family learning seems to be very successful as a promotional tool for widening participation in adult learning. Cara and Aldridge (2003) showed many different ways for it to be used to engage the community successfully as a part of a learning community, so tackling social exclusion in a non-threatening way.

Strategic planning should ensure that fund holders have the freedom to focus attention on the need to build capacity and manage available resources efficiently. Family learning has traditionally been funded by a variety of short-term, often project-based funding streams, which can make continuity of provision and consolidating progress difficult. Resource management is one of the key issues for multi-agency working: this must be a prime concern for all concerned in multi-agency collaboration and one that should also take account of the views of parents.

Points for reflection

Consider one of the case studies presented in the book, or a setting that you know well, in light of the following questions:

1. How well do early years staff know the local community? What measures have been taken to find out what is going on in the community?
2. Are parents fully involved in the learning of their children? If not, what actions can be taken to involve and include parents more?
3. Are early years staff confident that they communicate as partners with parents?
4. Do the early years staff in an establishment share their values and beliefs with each other and with the parents?

5. Is there a shared understanding between all agencies about the role of parents?

6. Is the funding for parent/family involvement transparent and regularly reviewed? Does any long-term strategic planning take into account short-term funding issues?

References

Alexander, T. (1997) *Family Learning, the foundation of effective education.* London: DEMOS

Atkin, J. and Bastiani, J. (1988) 'Are they teaching? An alternative perspective on parents as educators' in Cohen, A. (Ed) *Early Education, the Parents' Role. A Source book for teachers.* London: Paul Chapman Publishing

Atkin, H. and Bastiani, J. with Goode, J. (1988) *Listening to Parents: An Approach to the Improvement of Home-School Relations.* London: Croom Helm.

Blunkett, D. (2005) Europe is failing the skills challenge of India and China Keynote speech, *Learning Skills Council's Skills Summit:* 13th July 2005 www.dwp.gov.uk/

Bronfenbrenner, H. (1979). *The ecology of human development.* Cambridge, Massachusetts, Harvard University Press

Brown, G. (2005) Politics as a moral duty Speech by Chancellor Gordon Brown Labour Party *Conference: Monday 26 September 2005* http//:www.labour.org.uk/conference 2005

Cara, S. and Aldridge, F. (2003) *A Framework for the Engagement of Family Learning with Key Government Policies* NIACE

Dearing, R., National Committee of Inquiry into Higher Education (1997) *Higher education in the learning society, Main report* (The Dearing Report). London: [Stationery Office],.

Desforges, C. and Abouchaar, A. (2003) *The Impact of Parental Involvement, Parental Support and Family Education on Pupil Achievement and Adjustment: A review of literature,* DfES Reseach Report 433, DfES Sheffield

Department for Education and Skills (DfES) (2004) *Every Child Matters: the next steps* Nottingham: DfES Publications

Department for Education and Skills (2004) *Family Literacy, Language and Numeracy: a guide for policy makers,* DfES

Department for Education and Employment (1998) *The Learning Age: A Renaissance for a new Britain,* DfES

Department for Education and Employment (2001) *Skills for Life Strategy: The National Strategy for improving adult literacy and Numeracy skills,* DfEE

Department for Education (1994) *Our Children's Education – the Updated Parent's Charter,* DfES

Devereux, J. and Miller, L. (2003) *Working with children in the early years.* London: David Fulton HMSO (2003) *Every Child Matters.* Norwich, The Stationery Office

Dowling, M. (2005) *Young Children's Personal, Social and Emotional Development.* (Second ed.) London: Paul Chapman Publishing

Dyson, A. and Robson, E. (1999). School, Family, Community: Mapping School Inclusion in the UK. Leicester, Youth Work Press in collaboration with the Joseph Rowntree Foundation.

Haggart, J. (2000) *Learning legacies: A guide to Family Learning.* Leicester: NIACE

Istance, D., Schuetze,H.G. Schuller, T. (2002) *International Perspectives on Lifelong Learning: From Recurrent Education to the Knowledge Society.* Buckingham: Society for Research into Higher Education and Open University Press

Kennedy, H. (1997) *Learning Works. Widening participation in Further Education,* DfES

Lareau, A. (1989) *Home advantage: social class and parental intervention in elementary education.* London: Falmer

Mason, J. (2002) *Qualitative researching.* London: Sage

Moser, C., (1999) *Improving literacy and numeracy: a fresh start: the report of the working group chaired by Sir Claus Moser,* London: DFEE

National Evaluation Sure Start (2002) *Early Experiences of Implementing Surestart Report,* Nottingham: DfES Publications

NIACE (1995) *Riches beyond price: making the most of family learning.* NIACE

NIACE (2003) *Evaluation of LSC Funded Report on Family Learning.* NIACE

NIACE (2003) *A NIACE Response to the DfES' Consultation on the Green paper Every Child Matters* (Cm5860). NIACE

NIACE (2004) *Extended schools and adult learners* (briefing sheet 53) http//:www. niace.org.uk/information/Briefing_sheets

Nutbrown, C., Hannon, P., and Morgan, A. (2005) *Early Literacy Work with Families.* London: Sage

Ofsted (2000) *Family Learning: a survey of current practice.* London: Crown Copyright.

Ofsted (2001) *Ogley Hay Nursery School Report.* London: Office for Standards in Education

Passey, D. (2000). Developing home-school links: Implications for learners, learning, and learning support. InTaylor, H. and Hogenbirk, P. (eds.). *Information and communication technologies in education: the school of the future.* Kluwer Academic Publishers: Boston, MA. pp. 159-76

Penn, H. (2005) *Understanding Early Childhood. Issues and controversies.* Berkshire: Open University Press

Pugh, G. (1992) *Contemporary Issues in the Early Years.* London: Paul Chapman Publishing

Qualifications and Curriculum Authority (QCA) (2005) *Occupational standards for family learning.* London: QCA

Schuller,T. (2002) Lifelong Learning as the Social Construction of Knowledge *Lifelong Learning in Europe,* Vol. 17, No.1, pp33-40

Siraj-Blatchford, I and Brooker, E (1998) *Parent Parental Involvement Project in one,* London LEA. Research Report, University of London, Institute of Education

Siraj-Blachford, I. and Clarke, P. (2000) *Supporting Identity, Diversity and Language in the Early Years,* Berkshire: Open University Press

Sylva, K and Siraj-Blatchford, I. (1995) *The early learning experiences of children 0-6: strengthening primary education through bridging the gap between home and school.* Paris: UNESCO

Taylor, J. and Woods, M. (1998) *Early Childhood Studies. An holistic introduction.* London: Arnold

Tizard, B. and Hughes, M. (1984) *Young children learning: talking and thinking at home and at school.* London: Fontana

Weinberger, J., Pickstone, C. and Hannon, P. (2005) *Learning from Sure Start.* Buckingham: Open University Press

Notes on contributors

Dr Karen Clarke taught in various settings including early years, a special school, and also in further and adult education. She has worked for a charity for children with special education needs which specialised in education and training for staff and parents. Karen teaches on the Early Childhood Studies degree programmes and is Principal Lecturer responsible for the curriculum for the ECS, Special needs and Education Studies programmes in the School of Education, Wolverhampton University.

Bernadette Duffy (OBE) is Head of the Thomas Coram Centre in Camden, which has been designated as a Children Centre and identified as a particularly successful school in the Chief Inspector's report for 2004. The Centre offers fully integrated care and education for young children in partnership with their parents and local community and has a tradition of involvement in the arts. Bernadette was part of the Qualification and Curriculum Authority [QCA] Foundation Stage working parties for the Guidance for the Foundation Stage and 'Birth to Three Matters'. She is Vice-Chair of the British Association for Early Childhood Education, and has contributed to a number of publications. She is the author of *Supporting Creativity and Imagination in the Early Years and* co-editor with Gillian Pugh of *Contemporary Issues in the Early Years*.

Amanda French worked in adult education for over eighteen years as a tutor, manager and trainer. In FE she taught English Literature and Language and literacy based core/key skills and basic skills to adult learners from many different curriculum areas across a wide range of settings. She has also provided training to tutors, support workers from the college and a variety of other organisations such as probation, employment services and the voluntary community sector. She worked for the Workers Educational Association as Skills for Life co-ordinator, developing Skills for Life across a range of community learning programmes and curriculum areas, including accredited and non-accredited learning and NIACE as their regional development officer in Skills for Life. She is a senior lecturer in Early Childhood Studies and Education Studies at Wolverhampton University.

Jenny French has been Senior Lecturer at the University of Wolverhampton for six years but trained originally as a Paediatric Physiotherapist. It was in this role that she researched into Sensory Integration for children with DCD and introduced Sensory Integration Therapy into the UK from USA. She has worked with profoundly and multiply disabled children for many years in special and mainstream schools. Her first career change took her into the management of Child Health Services where she became interested in multi-agency working and social inclusion. She then joined an International Children's Charity working across Europe and eventually joined the Early Years team at the University of Wolverhampton. Her special interests are in promoting diversity and equality in line with the Every Child Matters agenda.

Janice Marshall trained originally as a nursery nurse (NNEB) and has worked in the Voluntary Sector, Social Services and Education for almost twenty years. She is currently the Deputy Head of the Thomas Coram Centre in Camden, which offers fully integrated care and education for young children. Janice takes the lead on Multi-agency working, parental family support, and parental involvement in the nursery. In July 2006 Janice successfully completed the National Professional Qualification in Integrated Centre Leadership (NPQICL) and is currently undertaking a Masters Degree (MA) in Early Years Education at the Institute of Education.

Margaret McCullough qualified as a social worker in 1990 and practiced for a number of years in a voluntary organisation, a maternity and paediatrics unit of a hospital, and a child and adolescent mental health service. She joined the Early Childhood Studies team at the University of Wolverhampton in 2003-2006. Margaret returned to social work practice in 2006

Martin Needham trained and worked as an Early Years teacher in Nottinghamshire, London and Pakistan. He then spent four years as an Early Years Development Officer for a local authority, working on a range of initiatives including Early Years Development and Childcare Partnerships, Children's Information Services, Foundation Stage, Neighbourhood Nurseries, Quality Assurance and Children's Centres. He became a senior lecturer in Early Childhood Studies at Wolverhampton University in 2003 and is undertaking research into forums that encourage parents and practitioners to exchange views about interactions with children aged 1 and 2.

Iram Siraj-Blatchford is Professor of Early Childhood Education at the Institute of Education, University of London. Her current research projects include: Evaluation of the Foundation Phase in Wales and the Effective Pre-school and Primary Education (EPPE) project, a major DfES ten-year study. She is particularly interested in undertaking research and writing which aim to combat disadvantage and give children and families from these backgrounds a head start. She is an advisor to Government and has worked for UNESCO and UNICEF. She is the co/author of over 30 books, monographs and major published research

reports and over a 100 scholarly chapters, articles and reports. She is visiting professor at the universities of Beijing Normal and Wolverhampton. She lives in
Cambridge with her husband John.

Faye Stanley worked in several early years settings in Birmingham, for Education
and Social Services departments and taught in a primary school for six years.
She is now teaching on an Early Childhood Studies Course, at the University of
Wolverhampton where she is module leader for the 'Birth to Three Framework'
and 'The 3-8 Curriculum'. Her research interests involve quality in early years
education and comparative education as well as barriers to children's learning.

Dr Judy Whitmarsh is a senior lecturer in the School of Education at the University of Wolverhampton. Her background is in school health and she was for many
years a school nurse and head of PSHE. With a mid-life career change, Judy
began academic study and qualified as a teacher and a counsellor. Her doctoral
thesis, located in a Sure Start area, investigated first-time mothers' understanding and knowledge of infant speech and language promotion. The difficulties that
arose from gaining ethical consent for cross-disciplinary research led to a deep
interest in ethical issues, further publication, and many conference presentations.

Jenny Worsley is a senior lecturer in Early Childhood Studies at Wolverhampton
University. Her background is embedded in early years education, primarily as a
practitioner working in a variety of early years settings, including community day
provision, schools, nursery and playgroups. Jenny's interest in the early years
stemmed from her own children's learning and development and the realisation
of the importance of proving quality care and education for young children. Her
research interests include the use of information technology in facilitating children's learning, pedagogical issues of children's play and issues relating to
professionalism within the early years.

Index

194501